It is essential to understand con[...] story, but some things are timeless and they weav[...]

Feelings are not constrained by era. Secrecy and societal shame were a huge factor in how 'wrong' this situation felt. It was wonderful that Molly's parents were open and understanding, and it certainly helped to integrate Molly's life when she was able to meld her past and her present and take them all into her future.

In my 45 years' experience working with families I find that adoptive families with both birth and adoptive children have an easier time with the open adoption factor and this was true for Molly's parents and family.

Fran is a great writer, and this is a great memoir. I hope that it reaches many and that it is as cathartic for everyone as it must have been for Fran to write it.

The perspective and voice of all of the birth/first parents is always essential. This voice is underserved and misunderstood. Thank you Fran.

> — JOYCE MAGUIRE PAVAO, EdD, LCSW, LMFT, Founder and CEO of Center for Family Connections, Inc.; Founder and Director of Riverside After Adoption Consulting and Training; author, lecturer, and consultant

The Story of Molly and Me is a deeply honest and intimate peek into an era prior to Roe vs. Wade, at the eve of the sexual revolution, when shame and blame were often the response to unwed pregnancy.

Fran Gruss Levin tells the emotional cost of living through the heartache of becoming pregnant by her high school sweetheart and surrendering her baby to adoption. A baby never seen—never forgotten.

I, too, shared this experience and was immediately transported back inside a world of crinoline skirts, high school proms and the passion of first love. Levin's ability to paint the colors and textures of innocence is profound. Our stories are all different and yet the same. She brings to life the cost of secrets and lies that resulted in living an unauthentic life until she claims her truth and finds the strength to tell *The Story of Molly and Me.*

> — PATTI HAWN, Entertainment Publicist, Author of *Good Girls Don't*

An important book that speaks to the issues of adoption, reunion, self-discovery and, finally, healing.

The Story of Molly and Me is a compelling memoir of a woman who sets out on a journey to find the child she surrendered to adoption as a teenager. I found myself totally caught up in the unfolding of Fran's past life, search, reunion and the discoveries of long buried secrets. Her raw and candid sharing of the emotional impact the loss of a child had in her life and the integration of Molly into her life and family, as well as the dawning sense of compassion and love she feels for Molly, should be a must-read for adopted persons as well as mothers of adoption loss and those who love them.

> — CAROL CHANDLER, Mother and Voice for Honesty in Adoption

The Story of Molly and Me

A Memoir

SECOND EDITION

Fran Gruss Levin

SUNNY SKIES PUBLISHING

Published by SUNNY SKIES PUBLISHING

Cover photo of Saugatuck Reservoir, Fairfield County, Connecticut
by Fran Gruss Levin

Back cover author photo by Phil Vadeboncoeur

Editing and design: Lesley Weissman-Cook
Lwc.Jhc@gmail.com

Photo editing: Jacob M. Cook
Jmwcook7@gmail.com

ISBN-13:978-0692864036
ISBN-10:0692864032

In loving memory of my grandparents, Irving and Ceil Brenner, my grandfather Abraham Gruss, my uncle Jay Brenner, my aunt Ethel Lesser, and my parents Anita and Martin Gruss. I also want to remember Nancy Zielinski, my dear friend, who kept my secret for decades, and left this life too soon.

ACKNOWLEDGMENTS

How do I begin to thank the many people who have loved and supported me throughout my life? There are many people I could name who were there for me at different times in my life, and there are some who have been consistently there.

I hold all of you dear. You were (and are) a significant part of my life and have shaped me into the resilient woman I am now. I have changed the names of some of the people in my past to protect their privacy, but that doesn't mean I don't think of you and thank you for the huge role you once played.

I especially want to thank my daughter, Molly Kramer Feder, for allowing our story to be told. I also want to thank my sons, Corey Levin and Jay Levin, for their love and encouragement. To my youngest child, Alexis Levin, I want to express my gratitude for being with me every step of the way. From the time you were eleven years old at the start of our search, you have been totally immersed and anxious to be part of our journey. To the fathers of my children, you will always hold a very special place in my heart.

Thank you to Bernard and Eileen Kramer for being such wonderful, loving and accepting people. You made a seemingly insurmountable situation into an opportunity to create a welcoming extended family.

I want to thank Jane Servadio, Carol Chandler, and the other members of Ties That Bind and Adoption Healing who shepherded me through the early years. My graduate school professors, who encouraged me to integrate my ongoing adoption research into every paper I wrote, deserve a mention as well.

A very special thank you to Eleanor Craig Green who was my sounding board, my mentor, and the one who asked all the right questions. You gave me the tools to put my life back together.

To my friends from Connecticut, and my new friends from South Carolina, who urged me to fulfill my dream of getting this book published, I am lucky to have had you by my side.

I can't leave out Donna Muro, who helped me remember so much, and Nadine Willig and Sandy Dressler Berman who provided their shoulders to cry on when I needed them. To Gail Burns and Patti Diamond, I appreciate your help in proofreading and the suggestions you made to make this story more readable. A huge thank you to Jane Lerner for her proofreading at the 11th hour because she just can't help it! Brava and thank you to Lesley Weissman-Cook, my amazing editor and book designer, my cousin, and my friend.

And to my husband, Phil Vadeboncoeur, your love and support mean so much to me. Your cheering me on through the process, your compassion when I was down, and your delight when I was up, allowed me to bring this story to fruition.

CHAPTER 1

Sweet Sixteen

*F*rom somewhere far off I heard the sound of my clock radio and knew it was time to get up for school. I thought about hitting the snooze button and going back to sleep for another ten minutes. However, it wasn't a good idea. Getting up at six o'clock in the morning was not my favorite activity, but I had no choice. Dad waited for me in the car until ten minutes past seven, and then he was off to work. If I didn't get out there in time to go with him, I was out of luck and would have to walk the three miles to school. Resolutely, I turned off the alarm and sat up in bed; it was still dark in the room, and I had to be quiet or I'd wake my eleven-year-old sister, Sidra. I quietly got up and tiptoed down the hall to the bathroom.

The light hurt my eyes as I turned on the switch. For a moment I couldn't see anything, and then I gradually began to focus. I sleepily leaned over the sink and looked into the mirror. Then it hit me. Today was my birthday. Friday, April 6, 1962. Today I was sixteen years old. A warm feeling flooded through me, and I smiled. I'd reached the magical age of womanhood.

Ironically, the face looking back at me in the mirror did not look much like that of a woman. Thin, high cheekbones, small, soft blue eyes, and short, curly brown hair framed my face. *Yuk,* I thought, and turned on the shower. I jumped into the steaming water, washed myself quickly, and hopped right out again. I had no time to waste.

I opened the closet and pulled out a delicately striped, yellow shirt-waist. I slipped it over my head and buttoned the pearl buttons up to the ruffled neck. I swished back down the hall to the bathroom where I brushed my hair, then put on some mascara and a little lipstick. *Not great,* I thought, *but it's okay.*

I looked at my wristwatch, discovered it was nearly seven o'clock, and stopped examining myself. I had to rush. I ran back to my room, stepped into three crinolines and my shoes, grabbed my books and hurried outside to meet my father. Mom would be sleeping late as usual, getting up just in time to get Sidra out the door to walk to school.

Dad was sitting in the car, the engine running, anxious to begin his day. Just forty years old, he was very handsome with his wavy dark brown hair and sparkling blue eyes. "Happy Birthday, honey," he said, smiling. "Are you ready for a big day? Do you have any tests? Is your homework all done?"

"Thanks, Daddy. Yes, I'm ready, and no, I have no tests . . . and of course my homework is all done."

Dad was a real perfectionist when it came to my schoolwork. Although I tried hard, the A grades didn't come easily. I needed to focus on my studies to get the grades Dad wanted to see, but I truly preferred talking on the phone, reading romance novels, or watching TV. However, Dad was relentless. Each night he grilled me, checking my math and quizzing me in science, until he was sure I understood the material. Often, I would end up in tears from pure frustration. I wanted so much to please him, to make him proud of me. At times, though, it seemed that no matter what I did, it wasn't good enough to satisfy him.

I loved being with my Dad, though, and the best part of being with him was talking together. He loved intellectual exercises and often presented the most absurd point of view, just to get me riled up. Mostly though, we talked about the world, about philosophy, about the quest for excellence, and about the traditions and heritage of our family and its relationship to history and the Jewish people. I was so in awe of his great intelligence and wisdom, and hoped that I could measure up.

We arrived at school on that brisk spring morning in plenty of time. Dad stopped at the light across from the high school. We gave each other a peck on the cheek and I hopped out of the car. Dad drove off, and I slowly and deliberately crossed the street. With the gentle breeze blowing on my face in the morning sunshine and my crinolines rustling, I walked majestically into the building, proud that it was my birthday, and excited to finally be sixteen.

Will Bill be around? I wondered, as a knot began to tighten in my stomach. Inevitably, the first person I saw was Bill, a boy I had recently dated and still liked a great deal. He gave me a nonchalant "Hi," and kept going. I felt the urge to burst into tears but managed to hold myself together.

Just then, I saw my friends Sue and Ennis, and I called out to them. "Wait up!"

"Great dress, Fran—Happy Birthday. I'm so excited about your party on Sunday. It's going to be really neat. So who's coming?"

"I don't know definitely, yet, but Ronnie and Tim are coming, and Laura and Pat. Jeff will be there, but I haven't heard from Bill."

"Don't worry about it," said Ennis. "He was a jerk to drop you."

"I know," I said, "but it still hurts. I really liked him a lot. He took me on my first date, and he was my first real boyfriend."

"The only reason he started seeing Mary was because she's easy," Sue quipped. "He knew he wasn't going to get past first base with you."

I wondered to myself if perhaps that wasn't a mistake—that if indeed I had let him get past "first base," he'd be with me now. I quickly rejected the thought. *I was a good girl, and good girls didn't let boys get past first base. The end!* The day finished without too much fanfare, and I spent the following day planning my party.

The Sunday weather was glorious. The crisp chill of springtime turned warm in the afternoon sunshine. Mom had done everything possible to ensure that my Sweet Sixteen was a beautiful affair. The backyard was dotted with rented tables and chairs, and food was carried on trays to the carefully dressed teenagers who sat like polite young adults chatting and joking. Friends from every venue of my life had come to celebrate with me. Not only were my friends from school there, but joining them were friends from the synagogue youth group, and Edie, my best friend from summer camp in New York.

I moved from table to table, nervous as could be, attempting to join in whatever conversation was going on. These were my friends, yet somehow I felt like I was on the outside, looking in. My hair was too short and too curly. I was too tall and too thin. My silk chiffon dress, which Mom said looked perfect, rustled when I walked, the starched crinolines creating the proper effect. Nonetheless, I wasn't too sure about the huge turquoise cabbage roses all over the white background. As usual, Mom had picked it out and bought it, disregarding my ambivalence.

The cake, baked by Dad's cousin Sally, was a masterpiece—beautiful and delicious. Ever the charismatic entertainer, Grandpa Irving walked around performing card tricks and other sleight of hand. My father stood proudly surveying the assemblage of well-behaved young people, and I basked in his approval.

But despite the success of my party, an overpowering sense of loneliness crept over me. I observed the closeness between the couples there, the easy way they related to one another, and wondered if I would ever be that lucky. I was missing Bill. Actually, I was missing the relationship with Bill that had never quite materialized. He and Mary were now going steady. I wanted so much to feel a closeness with someone with whom I could relax and be myself. It seemed so far out of my reach.

I wondered what was wrong with me—I couldn't seem to act naturally around boys. Even with my girlfriends from school, I often felt as if I was on the fringe of the social group. Could it have anything to do with my being Jewish while they were not? Sometimes it seemed like they belonged to some exclusive club of which I was not a member. Yet I didn't feel like I fit in with my Jewish friends either. I didn't know who I was or where I belonged.

I looked at my parents, who seemed so much in love. When they met at a college dance, Mom was seventeen and Dad was eighteen. He had been president of his high school senior class and was considered a "Big Man on Campus" in college. She was a beautiful college freshman, studying to be an actress. She had been dating since she was thirteen years old and had her choice of many young men who had crushes on her. When they married three years later, the summer after Mom's junior year in college, Dad had just graduated. In 1943, getting married was the only logical—and respectable—thing to do when you were in love.

They moved to Connecticut where Dad went into the retail lumber business with his father, my Grandfather Abe. Dad had wanted to be a civil engineer, but he was needed in the family business and now had the responsibilities of a married man, and so he put his dream aside. Mom had promised her parents that she would finish college, and she did this by getting on the train every day and commuting the hour to New York

City. She finished college right on schedule, and then went to work as a receptionist.

Mom's dream of becoming an actress soon took a back seat to her role as a wife. Mom and Dad bought their own home, and three years into their marriage, I was born. As I grew up, my parents often delighted in sharing with me how well they had orchestrated their lives. They bragged that they were both virgins when they married, and together had found out what it meant to share true love. They had planned each of my mother's pregnancies (two of which, sadly, ended in miscarriage). Their lives revolved around raising their two daughters with the same precise attention to detail with which they had planned everything else in their lives.

How could I ever live up to that model of casual perfection? I didn't know, but at sixteen, I believed I had spent my entire life trying. All I wanted from them was their approval—to feel that I was good enough for them. In my heart, I sensed that somehow I was not.

I went back to enjoying my party and my friends as best I could. I could only hope the future would hold something special for me.

CHAPTER 2
Boys

*I*t was the second Saturday in May, the day of the annual Roosevelt School Spring Fair. I planned to go with Ennis and meet some other girls there to ride the Ferris wheel, play some games of chance, and eat the wonderful greasy food. I was looking forward to the afternoon as an excuse to hang out with my friends, and of course to check out boys. The fair was THE place to be this afternoon, and I was excited. I got dressed carefully, putting on a pair of chino shorts and a white shirt with bobby sox and sneakers. I would look like all the other teenage girls there, and that would suit me just fine. I hoped we might bump into Bill. Perhaps if he saw me he would feel bad about dropping me and we could get back together.

When we arrived at the fair, there were throngs of people everywhere. We ate and walked around, all the time looking for people we knew. "Look, Ennis, here come Ronnie and Paul," I whispered.

Sure enough, walking right up to us were two boys our age whom we'd known since elementary school. Ronnie Stein had left the public high school and was enrolled in a private school nearby. With his friendly, open manner, he'd managed to meet lots of people I'd never met. We'd been friends most of our lives, and he was one of the few boys with whom I felt comfortable in conversation.

"Hi Fran, how are you?" I managed to utter a quiet hello back, ever conscious of his friend Paul, whose tall, shy good looks rendered me nearly speechless. Just then, two slightly older boys walked over.

"Hey, how's it going?" one of them said, looking right at Ennis and me. Ronnie made the introductions. "Ennis, Fran, meet Ken Jamison and Greg Smith."

I began to feel overwhelmed. Greg was somewhat short, had dark hair and twinkling eyes. It was obvious he loved meeting new girls. He smiled and made a remark about all the great looking chicks he'd managed to meet that afternoon. I thought to myself that he was a bit too sure of himself. Ken, on the other hand, was tall, thin, and soft spoken. His brown hair was cut short, but with a wave in front that had a habit of falling over his brow when he talked. A dimple marked his left cheek when he smiled. His brown eyes were soft and friendly.

Cheerfully, Ken spoke. "Hi girls, nice to meet you. Do you go to Norwalk High?"

Ennis answered, "We do. We're sophomores. How about you?"

Ken responded, "We graduated from NHS last year. We're finishing our first year at UCONN."

My God, I thought, *these guys are in college. They wouldn't be the least bit interested in a couple of sixteen-year-olds.*

Ronnie interrupted my thoughts. "Ken lives right down the street from Paul and me. We play basketball a lot over on the school playground."

Less than a mile away, I thought. *I'll have to start hanging out at the playground more.*

Greg elbowed Ken. "Come on, Ken—I've gotta be at work in a half hour."

"Okay," Ken replied. He turned to Ennis and me and gave us a warm smile. "It was nice meeting you. Hope I see you again." I shyly smiled back. As they walked away I turned quietly to Ennis. "Cute, huh?" "You bet," she replied.

Ronnie looked at me quizzically, poked Paul in the side, and said, "See ya girls."

I spent the rest of the afternoon hoping Bill would show up, but he never did. Darn, I thought. *Where is he? What is he doing? Everyone is here but him.*

Ennis was aware of my mood. "Fran, try to put him behind you." All I could think about was the big dance coming up at our friend Sue's club. All my friends were going. Would anyone ask me?

"What about the dance at the club?" I asked her.

"Don't worry," she said. "We'll all go to the dance and we'll have a great time."

CHAPTER 3
Summer Love

A few weeks later, Bill called. He and Mary had broken up. As we spoke, I tried to sound casual, but I believed that he was just being friendly and was no longer interested in me. It hurt so much. Yet, at the end of the conversation, he asked me to go out on a date. I accepted, but was confused and unsure of his reasons for asking me out.

The date was a simple, pleasant evening—but somehow disappointing, and unlike the comfortable and affectionate dates we'd had before. He brought me home and walked me to the door, saying good night without so much as a kiss.

The night of Bill's senior prom came and went. I wondered aloud afterward to my friend Sue. She told me she couldn't figure out why he hadn't invited me, because he'd been talking about it for weeks. Evidently the night we went out he was going to invite me, but lost his nerve. I guessed that he still cared for me, but something was in his way.

I worked up my courage and asked him to take me to the dance at Sue's club. When he said yes, I was elated. At the dance, Bill was moodier than I'd ever seen him. I danced with him, but we didn't talk much. As we strolled on the beach afterward, he held my hand. I yearned to know what he was thinking, but couldn't put my thoughts into words. When he took me home we lingered on the porch for a while. His kiss was brief and gentle. *Was he kissing me because he wanted to,* I wondered, *or because he thought it was expected of him? Did he feel anything at all for me?*

In my heart, I knew it was the last kiss he would give me. Three days later, Bill graduated and joined the Navy. I didn't expect to ever see him again.

School was over and the lazy days of summer were beginning. I was planning to work at a retail store and practice driving so I could get my license. One evening the last week in June the phone rang for me. It was Ken. My heart started racing nervously the way it always did when I started to talk with a boy. "I hope you remember me, Fran. We met at the Roosevelt Fair last month. I got your number from Ronnie Stein."

"Of course I remember you," I replied. Who could forget his soft brown eyes and shy smile?

"I was hoping you'd like to go to the stock car races with me in Danbury on Saturday night." I wondered if Dad would let me go, but I figured since Ronnie had introduced us, I could talk him into it.

"I need to check with my parents, but I think it would be okay," I offered, hoping I didn't sound infantile.

I would be on pretty shaky ground with Dad. An older guy, race cars, and a track forty-five minutes from home. This was not like going to the movies in town with Bill. Nonetheless, I somehow talked Dad into it!

Saturday night came and I nervously got ready, wondering what the night would be like. When the doorbell rang at five o'clock, I raced to answer it.

I let Ken in and brought him inside to meet my parents. Mom smiled and said, "Hi, Ken. Would you like to sit down?" This was more of a statement than a request. Dad studied him carefully.

"So tell me, Ken, where are you two going and when can I expect you to be back?"

"Well, sir," Ken said assuredly, "the stock car races are every Saturday night all summer. They hold them at the Danbury Fair Grounds. We'll be going with another couple, my friend Greg and his date. The races get over about eleven. Since it's about a forty-five minute ride, and allowing for traffic—I'd say we'll be back about midnight or a little bit after." He exhaled slowly and waited for Dad's response.

"That sounds reasonable, Ken. Please be on time. Fran's mother and I don't want to worry."

Ken and I both got up and walked to the door. He deftly opened it for me, and I walked through, feeling ever so grown up. This was going to be a perfect evening! As we entered the driveway, I looked at his car—a

A '56 Chevy just like Ken's.

black 1956 Chevrolet, obviously freshly washed and polished. He opened the passenger side door for me, and I slid onto the bench seat.

He closed the door and walked quickly around to his side of the car, opened the door and jumped in. He looked over at me, smiled, and said, "Ready?"

"Sure am," I replied. He turned the key, shifted into reverse, and expertly backed out of the driveway.

As he shifted into first gear he asked, "Want to turn on the radio?" He seemed so comfortable and relaxed that I immediately responded to the calming tone of his voice.

I turned on a radio station we both liked, and listened to the rock and roll music as we went to pick up Greg and then his date, Suellen. I knew Suellen from school, and though we didn't hang around together, I was surprised that she was dating Greg. The ride to Danbury was on a picturesque, rural road. It was beautiful countryside, and I commented to Ken how much I liked the trees and flowers. He looked over at me and asked, "Have you ever been up to the Saugatuck Reservoir?"

"No," I replied. "Where is it?"

"I'll take you up there some time. It's in Weston—an enormous lake, all forested, and we can go hiking nearby." He paused a moment, then added, "Do you like boating?"

"Absolutely," I said enthusiastically. "My Dad had a boat for years, and we used to go fishing and out to the islands in the Sound to swim." Ken seemed genuinely pleased that we enjoyed the same activities.

"We'll have to go out on my boat then, too," he said eagerly.

The four of us talked on the ride to Danbury about school, teachers, friends we had in common, and our summer vacation. Ken told me he worked at a local catalog store. People would save special stamps they got for buying groceries or gasoline. When they saved enough, they could trade them in for anything from stuffed animals to vacations. He told me he truly enjoyed working there.

One of the other employees was a boy I knew vaguely from school, and there was also an older woman, Mrs. Green, who worked there. Ken told me he really looked up to Mrs. Green, and felt he could talk to her about anything. I told him about my summer job at the jewelry counter in a local discount store, and what a whiz I was becoming at changing watch bands.

We arrived at the fairgrounds, where hundreds of cars and people were milling about. "Get ready for a long walk," quipped Ken.

"There are so many people here," I stated naively, feeling somewhat overwhelmed.

"Wait until we get to the stands. You're going to love this," Ken offered. The strong, pungent smell of gasoline, oil and exhaust permeated the air. Ken took my hand as we made our way through the crowd, past the ticket gate, and up into the stands.

I could not meet his eyes, and my stomach began its familiar flip-flop.

Oh, why, I thought to myself, *can't I just relax and enjoy myself without being nervous?*

We found seats, squished together in the crowded bleachers, and waited for the first race to begin. The cars roared onto the track and the announcer began describing who was driving which car. Certain drivers had a large following as evidenced by the roar of the crowd when their names were mentioned. Ken and Greg had a particular favorite from our hometown of Norwalk, and I somewhat self-consciously joined the cheering for him.

Four hours and several hot dogs and sodas later, the races were over. As Ken put his arm around me while we walked, I realized that I wasn't nervous anymore. We attempted to leave the parking lot, along with a myriad of other spectators. "This may take a while," he mused.

I didn't care. I was having a wonderful time, sitting next to this very special guy. We drove home quietly, listening to the radio. It had become particularly quiet in the back seat, and it didn't take me long to realize that Suellen and Greg were busy doing a lot of kissing. I didn't dare look, but every once in a while Ken would ask, "You two alive back there?"

We would get a grunt or "uh huh," for an answer, and we would laugh softly. Ken put his arm around my shoulders, moving it only to occasionally shift gears. When we arrived at Suellen's house, Greg got out of the car and walked her to her door.

Ken looked at me apologetically and said, "Those two were really going at it, weren't they?"

"I'm a little surprised they would make out with us right there," I marveled.

"Greg has no respect for girls," he stated. "He just wants to see how many notches he can get in his belt."

"Are you serious?" I asked.

"Yeah, I don't like it much, but he's a good friend. I would never put a girl in that position though—especially a girl like you."

I studied his face in the dim light from the dashboard. I wondered if this was a line. *No,* I thought. *He is truly serious. He's a nice guy, and he respects me.*

Greg jumped back in the car. "Okay, Kenny. Drive me home! That was really NICE!"

"Greg, cool it. Fran's not interested in your exploits." I smiled at Ken's protectiveness and settled into the warmth of his body next to me on the seat. We dropped Greg at his house, and proceeded on to mine.

"Right on time!" he exclaimed.

I returned, "You'll make lots of points with my Dad."

"I had a really great time tonight, Fran. I want to see you again. Can you go out another night this week?"

"I'll have to ask," I replied. "He's not very flexible when I have to get up and go to work early in the morning."

"Well, I hope you can, otherwise I guess I'll have to wait for next Saturday night, huh?" With that, he tilted my chin up to meet his gentle kiss. My heart was racing and I returned his kiss cautiously.

Just then, the porch light began flashing. It was my mother's signal that we had sat in the parked car long enough. "My mother," I said, embarrassed.

"Don't worry about it. I don't want you to get in any trouble with your parents," he said soothingly. We walked to the door and stopped. I looked up at him and he tenderly kissed me again. "I'll call you tomorrow, okay?"

"I'd love that," I responded, and went into the house.

The next morning at eleven o'clock, the phone rang. Sidra raced to answer it. "It's Ken," she said wide-eyed. "Wow, he must really like you—but I can't imagine why!"

"Shut up, he'll hear you," I cried, panicky, grabbing the phone from her. I took a deep breath, then whispered, "Hello."

"Hi, Fran. I promised I'd call, and here I am. I had a great time last night."

Eagerly, I replied, "I had a really good time, too." He went on. "Since it's such a beautiful day, I wondered if you'd like to take a ride up to the reservoir."

Beside myself with excitement, I tried to sound calm. "That sounds really nice. What time?"

"How about two o'clock?" he asked.

Being the good daughter, I told him I'd have to ask permission and asked him to call me back in half an hour. In those days, girls didn't call boys on the phone. It just wasn't proper. The boys were expected to do all the pursuing.

I knew it would take time to convince my parents to let me go. I'd hear the old routine: "Where are you going? How long will it take to get there? What will you do when you get there? Who else is going? What time do you expect to be back?" I knew they were concerned about me, but it always made me feel that if I deviated one iota from the plan, or wanted to do something on the spur of the moment, I was being dishonest. And I really wasn't a dishonest kid.

As far as daughters went, I was pretty good. I was a nice girl, and intended to stay that way. After all, it had been drummed into my head often enough. "Fran," Dad would say, "you can talk to us about anything."

I believed him, yet there were thoughts that ran through my head that I certainly could never share with him or Mom.

There were thoughts about the queasy feeling I got in my stomach when I read a romantic novel, or watched love stories at the movies. My stomach would churn, and I'd feel a tingling sensation in places I hadn't known I could feel. I would have dreams at night that left me feeling weak and yet excited at the same time—dreams that I was swimming under pale green tropical water, naked and free, not even needing to rest or breathe. I'd experience that same sensual feeling I'd had when, at twelve years old, my friend Lily and I got our hands on a clandestine copy of *Peyton Place,* and read all the parts about sex, turning down the pages so we could read them over and over again. No, I could definitely not discuss those feelings with my parents. I was a nice girl, and nice girls did not have those feelings.

I went into the kitchen where Mom was preparing brunch. Sunday brunch was always a big deal at our house. It was the one day a week we had breakfast together as a family. Dad worked every Saturday morning until noon, had a quick lunch when he came home, and then we all went our separate ways. They went out every Saturday night with friends, so Sunday was family day. We were treated to two family meals—brunch at home and dinner at a restaurant.

"Mom," I said guardedly. "That was Ken on the phone. He wanted to know if I could take a ride with him this afternoon."

My mother smiled. I could tell she was relieved that I had stopped mooning over Bill. "Where to?" she queried.

I told her, "There's a reservoir in Weston where they have hiking trails. We'll only be gone a few hours. I promise I'll be home in time for dinner."

Dad sat down at his customary place at the head of the table. "Just the two of you?" he asked warily.

"Don't worry, Daddy," I reassured him. "You know you can trust me, and Ken is a real gentleman." I was beginning to feel more sure of myself.

I must have sounded convincing, because my father nodded. "Okay. Just be sure you're home in time for us to go out for dinner."

"Thank you," I said gleefully.

Sidra was grinning. "Fra-an li-ikes K-en," she chanted irritatingly.

"Shut up, Sidra," I countered.

"Girls, knock it off," scolded my father.

When Ken called back and I told him it was okay, I could hear the pleasure in his voice. The time dragged endlessly until I saw his car pull up in the driveway. I resisted the overwhelming urge to run out the door to greet him. It was the custom for a young lady to allow the young man to call for her at the door, greet her parents, and escort her out to the car. With custom dispensed, we were soon sitting side by side and driving through the countryside.

Watching his hands, comfortable on the steering wheel and effortlessly shifting gears, I was embarrassed that nearly three months after my sixteenth birthday, I still did not have my driver's license. "Every time I get into the car to practice driving with my father," I confessed, "we end up fighting. He makes me so nervous that I dread going with him."

"How about a driving school? They'll teach you to drive, and won't make you nervous at all," Ken suggested. "Then, when you get the knack of it, I'll teach you to drive a stick shift. You can practice in my car." I looked at him. Ken was making future plans for us. I felt like I'd known him forever.

"What a great idea," I replied. "I'll call a driving school next week. I should have done it a long time ago."

Ken was helping me to feel more comfortable about myself than I'd ever felt before. His kindness to me was mystifying. Why was he attracted to me? Why was it all so effortless? I could finally just relax and enjoy myself. It was amazing.

I sighed and put my head back on the seat. He slipped his arm around me and pulled me closer. It felt so good to have him near me. He smelled of soap and freshly laundered clothing. I studied his closely cropped hair, slightly longer on top. I took in the shape of his mouth with lips that bowed slightly into points. I searched his gentle eyes with softly curling lashes. His madras plaid shirt and khaki pants were starched and pressed, and he wore boat shoes without socks.

"What are you looking at?" he asked teasingly

Modestly, I smiled. "You. I'm looking at you."

"You are pretty good to look at yourself," he countered, pulling me closer, and lightly kissing my cheek. As we drove, the forest became deeper, the landscape more rustic. "We'll be there soon," he said.

I watched in awe as the great beauty of the trees opened up in spots to reveal an enormous body of water. Ken eased the car into a spot on the side of the road and parked.

He took my hand and led me into the woods, following a path he'd undoubtedly traveled before. I could smell the unmistakable scent of evergreen and feel the soft padding of pine needles under our feet. The path wound around fallen trees as we made our way down a steep hill. We came to a clearing, and I looked up. In front of us was a broad expanse of boulders of every size, arranged in such a way that no human could have put them there. We climbed over the rocks to the magnificence of the waterfront. The reservoir stretched out for hundreds of acres, farther than we could see as it turned back on itself.

"Ken, I've never seen anyplace more beautiful than this!" I exclaimed. He beamed at my pleasure. "I knew you would like it." We sat on a boulder that had been warmed by the sun and spent the rest of the afternoon sharing the details of our lives.

Ken was the younger of two children. His sister was eight years older, and already married with children. His father had always worked for

Saugatuck Reservoir.

the phone company, and his mother worked in an office. He was the first in his family to go to college, and his goal of becoming an accountant made his parents proud. Ken was also a huge sports enthusiast, and loved playing basketball and baseball, though he never had much time to pursue them in earnest because of his work responsibilities. On his own, Ken had bought his car, paid his insurance, and paid for college. He had a few very close friends from high school, but was not much for partying. He dated one girl a year or so before, he told me, but it never developed into anything serious. He said she was very pretty and had a great personality, but their relationship had not been a close one.

I told him about the importance of friends in my life, but revealed that I never felt there was anyone to whom I was very important. I shared how much I loved children and how I had always wanted to become a teacher—until, of course, I had a family of my own. That had always been my primary goal. I wanted to get married and have children, I explained. Being a wife and mother would bring me the ultimate fulfillment.

We discovered we both enjoyed hiking and boating, and I was proud to tell him I knew my way around my father's little boat, and could even bait my own hook and clean the fish I caught. Ken told me he was pleased I was different from other girls—he could talk to me and I was able to listen, and my interests were more complex than being a fan of TV and movie stars. I had never been so at ease with a boy before. Without being aware of it, the afternoon had slipped away.

"I don't want to get on your father's bad side by bringing you home late," he declared. Back in the car, I sat close to him, feeling his warmth beside me, his clean smell flooding my senses. My body was tense with anticipation. Before he started the car, he leaned over and kissed me again, at first tenderly, then more urgently. I responded in kind, my heart racing. Simultaneously, we pulled away.

"We'd better stop," I said. "Yeah," he sighed.

We pulled into my driveway in plenty of time. Ken turned to me and asked, "Next Saturday night, the races again?"

"Wonderful," I said without hesitating.

"Great—and oh, the Fourth of July—I have my Dad's boat—we'll go out and watch the fireworks from the water."

"I would love that," I answered happily, knowing full well I would have to get permission for each outing from my parents. I had no doubt I would be able to deal with that. Again he kissed me, and I felt the familiar tingling inside me.

"I'll call you," he offered. I knew that he would.

After that, Ken called every evening. At seven o'clock the phone would ring, and we would talk endlessly.

Dad's rules did not allow dates on nights when I had work the next day, but when I didn't, Ken and I were free to spend time together—as long as I told my parents where we would be going, what we were doing, and when we would be back.

The Fourth of July brought perfect weather. I packed a picnic basket with sandwiches, snacks and soft drinks. I dressed conservatively in a pair of black corduroy Bermuda shorts and a white blouse. Ken warned me it might get chilly on the water at night, so I brought along a sweater as well. At about four o'clock, Ken and I drove to the marina where he kept his boat. His friend Ray met us with his date, and the four of us embarked. He navigated the boat as skillfully and cautiously as he drove his car. Ken moored the boat near an island, and while we ate our dinner, we watched sea gulls feed and other sailors enjoy the summer evening. As the sun began to set, we moved the boat again, and anchored at a spot where we could see the fireworks.

Ray and his date settled themselves in one corner of the stern, and Ken and I cuddled in the other. As I sat wrapped in his arms, looking up at the exploding sky, his affection enveloped me. I felt a satisfaction I had never experienced before, and wondered if I was falling in love.

The weeks that followed were perfect. I managed to learn to drive with an instructor with whom I felt less stressed than with my father. As for Dad, he was thankful that we didn't have to fight about the lessons anymore, and by the end of July, I had my license. Ken was happy for me. As promised, he allowed me to practice driving his stick shift in a local school parking lot, joking when the gears would make their horrible grinding noises if I didn't get the timing just right.

Weekday evenings were spent on the telephone, and weekends were reserved for going to the races and going out on the boat or to the reservoir. I met more of Ken's friends, and he met mine. We celebrated his nineteenth birthday, and I presented him with my first gift to him, a new shirt. Our separate worlds became one.

One weekend in August he invited me to go with his family to their vacation house in New Hampshire. His parents insisted that he go with them as he hadn't been there all summer. For the first time, my parents said that I couldn't go. Mom explained that it just wasn't right for me to go away with Ken, and as disappointed as I was, I understood and respected their decision. Ken reluctantly joined his family. We knew we would miss each other, but I also viewed it as an opportunity to spend some quality time with my girlfriends.

The following week, Ken called with a surprise. "I have tickets for us to go to a Yankees game on Saturday afternoon. Can you go?"

"That's so cool," I replied gleefully. I was beside myself because I had never been to a major league baseball game before.

"The Yankees are playing Detroit," he said. "Greg got the tickets. He's taking Suellen, and he'll drive. After the game we'll go to Greenwich Village for dinner. What do you say?"

"Oh, Ken, it sounds like a perfect day! Let me convince my parents and I'll let you know tomorrow, okay?" To my amazement, it didn't take too much to convince my parents this would be an appropriate outing. They could obviously see how happy I was and that I was ready for what I perceived to be a very grown-up experience—a day in New York City.

The weather was cloudy and humid on Saturday, but that didn't dampen our enthusiasm. Ken and I cuddled in the back seat of Greg's car. I heard Greg bragging to Suellen about something or other, and as I scrutinized the back of his neck, I felt a wave of revulsion. Ken sensed my displeasure and whispered to me, "Fran, are you all right?"

"I'm okay; it's just that his attitude makes me sick," I confided.

"Just ignore him," Ken offered. "Let's just concentrate on us, and what a great day we're going to have together. Besides, I have a present for you."

With that, he pulled a box from the floor by his feet. I opened it gingerly, not knowing what to expect. I grinned as I pulled from the box a little stuffed monkey with a silly expression on its face. I laughed and kissed him. "Thanks, Ken, I love him."

He was right about the day we would have. Despite the clouds, the humidity, and my growing dislike of Greg, the game was exciting. The grass was so green, the lights so bright, the score board so huge . . . I could never have imagined I would enjoy a baseball game so much. After the game, we cheerfully headed to the subway to go to Greenwich Village to cap off a Yankees win.

As we emerged from the subway station, we noticed a light rain had begun to fall. We walked, hand in hand, to a little Italian restaurant, allowing Greg and Suellen to go on ahead of us. Just outside the restaurant, Ken stopped walking. He turned and looked down at me, his eyes tender and gentle. He put each of his hands on my shoulders, drawing me to him as he kissed me, lightly at first, then more deeply. A shiver went through me as I responded to him, my arms reaching up to feel his closeness. My face was wet from the rain, but the chill was gone as I returned the emotion. "Fran, I love you," he said ardently.

Surprised by his declaration, I pulled away from him, and searched his eyes. He repeated, "I love you." I knew then he truly did love me.

"I love you too," I responded. We kissed again—the kiss of best friends, smiling, content in the knowledge that we had found each other. Arm in arm, joyful at our confession, we entered the restaurant.

Returning home that night in the back seat of Greg's car, we sat enmeshed in one another. I felt so safe with him, so cherished. We kissed and gently explored the "safe" parts of our bodies. We knew instinctively that certain kinds of petting were off limits, and Ken did not push it. My heart pounded fiercely, and I felt it in my chest, in my head, and between my legs. Every so often we would stop, separate, and breathe deeply, then laugh at the recognition of our sexual boundaries. When he walked me to my door, we again embraced. "I love you so much, Fran," he said.

"Frizzy hair and all?" I asked.

"Frizzy hair and all," he declared. "I'll call you tomorrow."

Three weeks later, we had to come to terms with the fact that summer was over. I was headed back to high school, he back to college. As we sat in his car, the radio was softly playing the Duprees' You Belong to Me.

"I'm going to miss you so much while I'm away," he said wistfully. "But I'll be home every weekend to be with you, I promise. I'll leave after my last class Friday, and be back in time to pick you up from school at two-thirty."

"I'll miss you too," I answered. "I'll write you every day, and you can call me once during the week. We'll do just fine."

"This will be our song," he said. "Don't forget that you belong to me, always. I want you to wear my ring." He pulled his class ring from his finger and handed it to me. I took it and clutched it in my hand.

"Ken, I love you, but my father will never allow me to go steady with you. He doesn't approve of going steady at our age, and he'll really give me a hard time." The irony of my parents' being about our ages when they started dating was not lost on me. However, I knew that they were already in college at the time, and times were very different.

Reluctantly, he took the ring back. "Okay for now," he said, "but I'll be offering it to you again."

"Don't worry," I said. "I do belong to you, and a ring won't change that one way or another, despite what my father believes." With that, I began to cry, and he held me tightly, fighting back tears of his own.

CHAPTER 4
Floating

*A*nd so, we both began a new school year. I was a high school junior, and Ken a college sophomore. We worked into a routine of writing back and forth daily during the week, and spending whatever time we could together on the weekends. We celebrated our ongoing relationship as an achievement, marking the "anniversary" of our first date on a monthly basis. Last summer, the only thing we had ever disagreed about was my growing boredom with the races every Saturday night, and my wish to spend more time with my high school friends. When the races finally ended for the season, Ken agreed to do more things that I was interested in, like going to the movies and attending parties.

We would spend many Saturday nights babysitting for my sister so my parents could go out. On those nights, we would camp out on the living room sofa and watch TV, or on occasion we would play cards or board games with Sidra. Sometimes she would have a friend sleep over as well, and they acted as built-in chaperones, preventing our necking from going too far. Ken would stay until my parents came home. Then they would go to bed, and we would have to say goodnight.

Whether we had been out for the evening, or simply enjoying an evening at my home, saying good-bye was always difficult. Our kisses would become more urgent, the passion more intense. Drawing the line at where to stop became more confusing.

My mother was aware of the depth of our feelings and was worried about me. "Fran," she cautioned, "your father and I want to make sure you understand how important it is to see lots of different boys before you get married. You're so young to be with just one boy. That's why Daddy and I don't want you to go steady."

"I understand, Mom," I replied, "but I like being with Ken more than any other boy."

"Marriage is such a difficult thing, honey, without bringing religious differences into the relationship. You know we would never approve of you marrying someone who wasn't Jewish," she warned.

"But Mom," I challenged, "we're not that religious, and it's not that important to me. I know my heritage, and religion doesn't seem to be a big part of our lives."

"Fran," she continued. "You may not understand this now, but it is very important, and I'm asking you to promise me that you will never marry out of our faith."

"Okay, Mommy. Don't worry." I answered, not really understanding at all.

Later, Ken and I discussed the issue of our different religions. We had both been aware when we started dating that this might be an obstacle. However, neither of us expected that our relationship would be adversely affected by those differences, and anyway, marriage seemed very far in the future.

When the movie *West Side Story* opened that fall, Ken and I went to see it. Somehow, it became a paradigm for our relationship—two young people from different cultures in love. We admired the courage of Tony and Maria, and believed that in our suburban, sheltered world, we would be able to sensibly handle our cultural differences.

As our relationship deepened, so did my growing guilt about the feelings I would have when we were petting. At the end of an evening together we would go park at the beach. The parking spaces overlooking the water were always occupied on weekend nights by young sweethearts.

Occasionally, when Ken's parents weren't home, we would go to his house to be alone. I was never nervous with Ken, and I trusted him totally. I knew he would always stop when I asked him to. It was my own feelings that confused me. I loved Ken, and loved the physical sensations that coursed through my body when I was close to him. Yet I knew in my heart that my parents would not approve of the way we kissed, or how I allowed him to touch me in places no one had ever touched me before.

"Fran," he told me over and over when we said goodbye, "every time we're together, I never want to leave you. I've never loved a girl or felt so close to her as I do with you. If you ever told me to go away for good, I wouldn't be able to be with anyone else. You're the one that I really love—nobody has ever made me as happy as you do."

I would close my eyes when we kissed, imagining I was floating. It became our private game—kissing to float—and served as a distraction from our physical need for one another. We were aware that some of his friends were "going all the way." In Connecticut, at that time, contraception was against the law. Ken would joke about how one or another of his friends would be keeping the local smoke shop in business by buying illegal protection. Together we read a book about birth control and physical intimacy. We were fascinated by the sexual world that was so close but so far away. "That's not for us right now," Ken affirmed. "Going all the way should be reserved for marriage, and I would never ask you to do that."

"Besides, there are only two things I want or need right now, and they are you and an education. Fran, I want to transfer out of UCONN next semester and live at home where I can be close to you. I don't want to be an accountant. I want to be a teacher. They have the program I need at Southern Connecticut State College. I can commute there, work more hours, and see you or talk to you every day."

He's coming home to be nearer to me? I thought. *He loves me so much.* Even though I was somewhat ambivalent about being tied down at sixteen years old, I loved him for his sensitivity, his focus and his intelligence. I loved the way he smelled, the way he dressed, the way I had to stand on tiptoe to kiss him, the way I fit under his arm. Most of all, I loved being so adored by him.

One Sunday, when the foliage was golden and had begun falling from the trees, we traveled to the reservoir to walk and talk as we often loved to do. The leaves crunched under our feet, and the forest had the dusky smell unique to autumn. Ken ran over to a tree and turned to me, exclaiming, "This one is perfect!" With that, he took a pen knife from his pocket and began carving our initials in the trunk.

"Kenny," I admonished him. "You shouldn't do that!"

"I love you, and this means that a part of us will be here forever!" he shouted joyfully. "And we'll always know that today was a special day for us." He kissed me gently, took my hand, and led me the rest of the way up the path.

Sometimes Ken would remind me that he wanted to spend the rest of his life with me. He would say, only half joking, "Let's get married this weekend. I have about twenty dollars. We're old enough to get married in Maryland or North Carolina. We can go for the day, then zip right back home!" In more serious moments he promised, "I never want to love anyone else. I would never break up with you. If our relationship ends, it will be because you made it happen."

I was always aware of the eventual fate of our relationship, based on the promise I had made to my mother. I tried to reassure Ken, "No matter what happens, I will always love you."

By late fall, the guilt about my rising passion compelled me to go on a "reform" movement. "No more beach for a while, no more petting, no more going to your parents' house. I feel too guilty," I stated unequivocally.

Ken protested, "There's nothing wrong with our expressing our love for each other. It's normal and natural. But I'll do whatever you want. I don't want to lose you."

I would have dreams about making love with Ken, dreams where I floated to the logical conclusion of my desire for him. Ken would dream often of me, too, and we would share theses dreams with each other. Somehow we were able to express in words our mounting frustration, and Ken never forced me to go further after I told him to stop. The frustration would take its toll in other ways, however.

I began fighting more often with my father. It was so hard to concentrate on my schoolwork, and Dad was relentless in his efforts to make me into an outstanding student. No matter what I did, it was never good enough. He was critical of the amount of time I was spending with Ken, and yet there was no concrete reason he could offer for not allowing me to go out. One night, after coming home from a date with Ken, I found my father waiting for me in the kitchen. He began yelling at me, so loudly that Ken could hear him through the door.

Ken told me how upset he'd been by what he heard. "I wanted to come back in there and defend you, but I was so afraid that he'd make us break up, or I'd lose it and punch him. I figured it would be better for both of us if I was just here for you. Honey, no matter how rough the situation becomes, just remember, we've got each other—I'll never leave your side, I'll always be near. I never knew what true love was before I met you, and I don't want anyone to stand in the way of your happiness. That's the most important thing."

With the approach of the Chanukah and Christmas holidays, the differences in our religious backgrounds became more obvious. Ken had almost no knowledge of what Judaism was all about, and I felt, as always, like an outsider in the rest of the world's preparation for Christmas. I identified strongly with my heritage, even though our family was not particularly observant. It seemed right, however, that Ken and I would exchange gifts to honor our feelings at this time of year.

While I was sure that I loved Ken, I still felt conflicted about how much of a monopoly he had on my time. One Saturday night, when my friend Sue invited me to a party at her house at the same time Ken wanted to go to a basketball game, we decided to spend the evening apart.

I went to the party at Sue's, feeling liberated, yet at the same time feeling there was something missing. As the evening got underway, more and more teenagers piled into her house. The party was wonderful. It was good to see friends and have conversations with boys, too. I had a newfound sense of social competence, and it was refreshing to exercise it.

As I looked up from a conversation, I was shocked to see Bill walk in. I had no idea he would be there. He made his way toward us and joined the conversation. My stomach was in knots. "Well, hi there, Frani," he chortled.

"Hi Bill," I managed to squeak out. "How's the Navy?"

"Great," he grinned. "It's good to see you; you look nice." We chatted some more and soon found ourselves alone.

"Let's go sit down somewhere and catch up," he said.

"There aren't a whole lot of places to sit," I replied, as we picked our way through the throng of people. "Looks like the only available space is on the stairs."

So we sat side by side on the staircase, facing the front door. It gave us a good view of who was coming and going, and the action at the party. Bill filled me in on what life was like for him in the Navy, and how he had enjoyed the last six months. He didn't speak at all of our previous relationship, but as we talked he took my hand and held it. It seemed like an innocent enough act, and held no implications. It felt good, yet disloyal to Ken at the same time.

The front door opened yet again, and standing in the doorway—looking directly at Bill and me—was Ken. Our eyes locked, and his look changed to one of dismay as he saw Bill and our linked hands. "Ken," I exclaimed, "what are you doing here?"

"The game was boring, and I missed you. I thought I'd spend the rest of the evening with you. Guess that wasn't such a good idea," he replied despondently. "It looks like you're having a pretty good time without me," he stated with an edge of anger as well as hurt.

Part of me railed that I couldn't spend one evening socializing without feeling as if I had betrayed him. Yet the other part of me truly loved Ken for himself. The thought of hurting him was unconscionable. I pulled my hand away from Bill's and stood up. "Kenny," I returned, "it's not like that. Bill and I were just catching up. Please don't leave."

"I can't stay here, Fran. I'll talk to you some other time."

"Please, Kenny. Let's talk now," I begged. His voice rose as did the anger within him.

"Not now, Fran. Enjoy yourself with your friends." Before I could think of what else to say, he was gone. I wanted to smooth it over, to make it all right. I never intended to hurt him or be disloyal. I only wanted to be with my other friends, to spend an evening with kids from my high school and enjoy the casual flirtation with Bill. What was wrong with me? How could I love Ken and still want to have a life apart from him? As confused as I felt, I knew that I did love Ken, and I didn't want to lose him.

He called the next afternoon. Our conversation was stilted and cold. "I'm driving back to school this afternoon," he said. "I guess we won't have time to get together."

"Kenny, I'm sorry about last night. It was nothing between Bill and me, honest."

"Fran, I guess I'm selfish when it comes to you. I'm only happy when I'm with you, and I don't feel right when I'm with other people. I just want you for myself." I could hear the agony in his voice. "I wish we had more time to talk, but I've got to go. I'll write you, and maybe call during the week. Don't worry about it."

I had a sinking feeling in my stomach. I wanted to see him, hold him in my arms and tell him it was okay, but his anger and pain made him seem so far away. "Please be careful, Kenny, I'll see you next weekend. We're okay, honey, honestly," I declared—as much to convince myself as to reassure him.

On Tuesday his letter arrived.

> *Darling,*
>
> *The trip back to school was a nightmare. I got into a car accident in Hartford. Some guy rear-ended me on the highway. Nobody was hurt, but I ended up at the police station there for two hours. Then I still had to drive an hour from there back to campus. When we got back, we couldn't open the trunk to get the luggage out, so we had to take out the whole back seat. All this time, I'm thinking of you and that fight we had, and how all I want to be doing is working things out with you. It nearly drove me nuts.*
>
> *I know that you want more room to see other people, more freedom. I suppose the difference in our age accounts for a lot of that. When I was your age I wanted to see lots of different people, but now all I want is one person—you. I guess I love you too much. I've tried to love you less, but I can't. I've talked to Mrs. Green about our relationship, and she says she's noticed the change in me, for the better. She says I'm a nicer person now than I used to be. Maybe losing you is some kind of punishment for the inconsiderate things I've done in the past. The thought of being without you would be the most unbearable punishment; it hurts so much to even think about it. I hope that if this is the end of our relationship that I hold more of a place in your heart than just another name on the list of boys you've gone out with. If we do break up, I promise you I'll never discuss with anyone what we've done together. That's just between us. You're a good girl, and I wouldn't ever want anyone to take advantage of you.*

I cried as I read his words. He was so thoroughly devoted to me. He loved me so much, and I had treated him so poorly. If I loved him as much as I professed to, then how could I be so disloyal to him? I vowed never to hurt him like that again. I did love him, and wanted to reassure him of that.

His letter continued,

> *If you ever have any problems, just call on me . . . no matter when, where, how or what the nature of your problem . . . remember I'll always be there. I can't even imagine not loving you in the future—even if we're not together, I'll still love you.*

With all my heart, I believed every word of what he told me, and I wanted to make that pledge to him as well.

After that, I felt much less uncertain, and stronger in my commitment to Ken. The fact that my father had by now imposed limited hours when Ken and I could spend time together seemed to have backfired. I still felt guilty every time we would express our feelings physically, and nothing Ken said could reassure me.

"Frani, I love you so much and I want to express it. I don't see the need to 'go all the way.' In one way, I love you so much I would like to do it, but then again I love you so much that I wouldn't. Whatever you say, whatever you want is okay. I just never want to lose you."

"Kenny," I answered, "I love you too, and never want to lose you either." We got even closer emotionally. We were, in every way, best friends. He told me how beautiful I was on the inside, as well as on the outside. We communicated with one another freely, and with understanding. We worried about each other, were happy to be together, and wanted the best for the other.

Ken had done well during his time away from home. At school he became the captain of his dorm's basketball team. It gave him an outlet for his physical energy, and he was so good at it that it was a perpetual boost to his self-esteem.

He began to talk more frequently and seriously about getting married the year after he graduated from college. "By then, I'll have a job, be working on my master's, and I'll be able to support you and a family," he told me. "Transferring to Southern Connecticut will allow me to keep working, save some money, and be near you," he often said. "I still want to go steady with you, to declare ourselves openly, but I understand about your parents, and why we can't."

I continued to fight with my father often. He rarely allowed me to see Ken more than once every weekend. He still hammered away at me to date other boys, spend more time with my friends, and encourage Ken to date other girls. He was clear about the prohibition of going to the drive-in movies or parking at the beach. I wondered how obvious my heightened sexuality was. I would half-heartedly communicate all my father's stipulations and concerns to Ken, trying to convince us both that my father knew what was best.

Ken wouldn't hear of it. "I understand," he said, "but I won't go out with other girls. I love you, and I'm not interested in being with anyone else.

CHAPTER 5
Unconditional Acceptance

*A*s New Year's Eve marked the start of 1963, Ken and I went to a party at the home of one of my friends. Ken didn't often enjoy high school parties—they were noisy and juvenile by his standards—just an excuse for kids to drink or make out. But this New Year's Eve was different. It was the best one either of us had ever spent. My friends were amiable, Ken and I were in love, and the future seemed bright. As we kissed at the stroke of midnight, we were blissfully happy. We were together to greet a New Year—a year that we could not know would bring unfathomable changes.

Shortly after New Year's Eve, Ken went back to UCONN to take his final exams. He would soon begin the spring semester at Southern Connecticut, only forty minutes away.

Greg, who had some time ago picked up on my dislike for him, attempted to sabotage our relationship. Ken had befriended a girl named MaryAnn at school. Greg told Ken, "This girl MaryAnn is something else; if you don't go after her, then I will."

Ken was concerned, and told me about her. "Honey," he began, "MaryAnn is really sweet. She reminds me a lot of you. I think she likes me, but I don't want to go out with her because I love you. The problem is, if I don't do something, Greg will put the moves on her, and a nice girl will succumb to his scummy charm. I want to warn her about Greg, and I don't want to hurt her or see her hurt."

"Just tell her," I urged him. "Take her for coffee or something; I trust you to do the right thing."

"I don't know if it will do any good," he said. "But, I have to try. Greg is bad for anyone to go out with. I'd hate for someone like you to be embroiled in an affair with anyone who treats a girl like he does."

Ken made his coffee date with MaryAnn, and explained things to her. She said that she understood and thanked him for being a friend. I was truly gratified that Ken was honest with me. There was never a time I questioned his honesty and sincerity.

Finally, Ken moved back home. He worked days at the catalog store, went to school four nights a week, then would call, exhausted when he got home. We would talk until my father scolded me to get off the phone and go to sleep. I basked in Ken's love for me. As long as he was around to support me, I could handle my father's displeasure.

The pressure, however, did take its toll. Both my parents took every opportunity to point out the differences in our social and religious backgrounds. Ken and I talked about this problem often, and yet postponed taking action to some indefinite time in the future.

"Fran," he said, "I realize that I may have no future with you because of our different religions, but I still can't stop loving you . . . You know, my mother told me that she loves you very much and she wishes you were a religion somewhat similar to ours . . . it would make things so much easier for us. But we won't have to worry about that for a while I guess, so we can still keep as close as we are and still keep loving each other, all right?"

Early in February, Ken called, excited. "Frani, it's going to be Winter Weekend at UCONN. I really want us to go. It will be terrific. You can meet my friends, and we can go to a jazz concert, a basketball game, and other stuff. I'll stay with my old roommate Neil, and you can stay at one of the girls' dorms. What do you think?"

"Oh, Kenny," I gushed. "It sounds marvelous." The idea of a college weekend seemed so civilized, so adult. Some of my friends had gone on college weekends, and they had reported how spectacular they were. "I'll try to convince my parents. Wish me luck!"

Luck was certainly more than I needed. Mom thought it would be a nice idea. I figured she was thinking back to her own days in college. She tentatively said yes, and we planned what I would need to bring, including a new dress for the concert. That was a big mistake. Dad was furious at Mom for granting me permission to go without consulting him. He blew up at both of us.

"How could you give permission to her without discussing it with me first?" he bellowed at her. "Well fine, you two make your plans, and include me out!"

With that, my father began a marathon of shutting us out by not talking to us or acknowledging our presence. Whenever we would try to approach him, he would glare at us, then turn away and ignore us. The only time he would address us was to ask to have the ketchup passed at dinner, or to inform us when he was going out. Dad retreated into his own solitary world that did not include us. Because she had not done anything to incur his wrath, Sidra was the sole beneficiary of all Dad's affection, and that made his anger at my mother and me all the more painful. It must have made Sidra feel incredibly guilty.

I refused to allow my father's anger to mar my excitement at visiting UCONN with Ken. Mom and I shopped and packed, and the weekend came. As Ken and I left, Mom ushered us off wistfully, encouraging me to have a wonderful time. Sidra hung back, afraid of taking sides in the family battle, while Dad totally ignored my departure. I snuggled next to Ken in the car. With him, I felt safe, loved and accepted. He would never cause me the pain my father had at his rejection. Ken loved me unconditionally.

When we arrived, I settled into the dorm with two girls who were friendly and hospitable. They knew Ken from his time at UCONN. "So, you're Ken's famous girlfriend," they cooed. "We understand you're something special." I glowed, and I did feel special that Ken had made no secret of the fact that he had a girlfriend at home. Ken ran to his room to put his things away, and then came back to get me for a quick pizza at a local hangout followed by the basketball game.

The gymnasium smelled of polyurethane, and glared with the brightness of all the lights. The bleachers were enormous, and we made our way to our seats amid throngs of young people. The game began and I saw Ken's excitement. He loved two things—me and basketball! The squeaking of the sneakers on the court, the sound of the buzzer and the referees' calls were scintillating and remain etched in my mind. After the game, we were exhausted. Ken took me back to the dorm and kissed me warmly at the door. I went upstairs and promptly fell asleep.

The next day, well rested, we walked around the campus, went to a few shops, and bought souvenirs. I picked out a record album—featuring the bossa nova style that was so popular at the time—that I knew my mother and father would both enjoy. I hoped that proffering this token of peace and showing Dad I was considerate of his feelings would help his anger subside.

After Ken brought me back to the dorm to prepare for the evening, I dressed carefully in the new dress my mother and I had picked out. I looked in the mirror at the young woman in front of me. I was pretty! Reassured, I made my way downstairs where Ken waited in the lobby. I gazed at him and smiled. He was so handsome in his suit and tie. His hair was perfectly combed, and he looked at me with eager anticipation.

"You are so beautiful," he said adoringly, and bent to kiss me. His lips lingered on mine, and chills went through me.

"Wow, we better get out of here," I declared.

The auditorium was huge, and on the stage stood a solitary grand piano. "Ladies and Gentlemen," the master of ceremonies began, "may I present—Ahmad Jamal." The crowd applauded enthusiastically, and a man walked to the piano and sat down. He took his time, and when the crowd quieted, he deftly put his fingers down and began to play. I had never heard music like this before. The frenetic angst of the jazz piano was totally new to me. I was excited and confused by the cacophony, yet I knew that the man performing was a living legend. I reveled in the milieu of a college auditorium, surrounded by thousands of young adults, and was thrilled to be one of them. I looked at Ken, so handsome and self-assured, and felt confident about myself and about us.

When the concert was over we drifted out to his car. The night was freezing cold, and I cuddled close to him, hoping to get some warmth. He turned the key and the engine turned over. We sat shivering in the car, waiting for the heat to come on, the radio tuned to a favorite station. Ken pulled me closer and kissed me deeply. I responded with equal intensity. Silently, still holding me close, he put the car in gear, and we drove, without the need to speak, to a secluded area.

Finally, he spoke, "This is the apple orchard I told you about." I remembered Ken had written me about this spot as the place where UCONN students went when they wanted to be alone. He pulled the car into a spot far enough away from the other cars that we would have privacy. He put the engine in neutral and set the brake. We began kissing, declaring our love for one another, and allowed the growing passion within us to build.

"I want you so much, Frani," he declared fervently.

"It's all right, Kenny, I want you too."

"Honey, are you sure?" he answered in disbelief.

"I'm sure," I affirmed.

"I promise I won't hurt you. You won't be sorry. I love you, I love you," he swore.

On that bitter cold February night, I entrusted Ken with my love, my virginity, and my life. "Are you okay, Darling?" he asked apprehensively.

"Yes," I murmured, the warmth of his affection protecting me.

"Now you really do belong to me," he whispered lovingly, quoting the tune we thought of as "our song."

"I do belong to you Kenny. I love you so much, and I always will," I assured him.

The song "Tonight, Tonight" came on the radio. "That song reminds me so much of us," he said. "I always think of you and me when I hear it."

"I do too," I agreed. "I'm okay, really."

"It's almost curfew," he reminded me. "I'd better get you back to the dorm or you'll get locked out!"

We drove back to the dorm, and he walked me to the door. "Never forget how much I love you," he repeated, and kissed me again so that I had no doubt about his feelings for me. Nothing bad could ever come from a love like this. I went upstairs to the room where I was staying. My two roommates were already there—I wondered if they could guess what I had done, just by looking at me.

"Have a good time tonight, Fran?" one asked. The other girl laughed. Did she see? I wondered.

My God, I thought, *do they think I'm a slut?* I admonished myself. *Don't be ridiculous, Fran. They can't possibly know.*

"Yes," I replied. "I had a wonderful time, but I think I got my period. Do you have any supplies?"

"Too bad," the second girl answered. "Sure, I'll get some for you," and she gave me what I needed. I went into the bathroom and examined my blood-stained panties. This was not my period, I realized. I had just lost my virginity, and this was the confirmation of that fact.

Ken and I had reached a turning point in our relationship. I no longer had any doubt about my feelings for him. Despite my father's unwillingness to accept the depth of our commitment, it was a fact. Ken had always accepted me unconditionally. No matter what I said or did, he still loved me and wanted me. I had never experienced love like this, and it empowered me. I felt secure.

Unfortunately, my father remained angry and cold. I missed the closeness Dad and I had shared—the talks, the affection. I felt heartbroken that I had to lose one love in order to have the other one.

My physical relationship with Ken continued. Once we had tasted the supreme closeness of making love, there was no turning back. We searched for opportunities to be alone. Sometimes in the afternoon after school, while his parents were at work, we would go to his house. Occasionally we would even steal forbidden moments in the alcove near my kitchen door. I felt guilty about deceiving my parents, but my need for attachment and intimacy with Ken drove me.

CHAPTER 6
Promises

For my seventeenth birthday, Ken presented me with a special gift. Over a restaurant dinner, he handed me a little box. My fingers jubilantly opened it to reveal a charm for my gold bracelet. It was a circular pendant about the size of a nickel to which was attached a rose with two small rubies. Inscribed on it were the words, "I Love You."

"It's perfect, Kenny. I will treasure it, always."

"Sweetheart," he said, "we have had some tough times, but I wouldn't change one moment of our time together. It's been almost a year now, and I'm sure if we can make it that long, we'll be able to make it forever. I hope . . . that we will love each other much longer."

"Kenny," I agreed, "I can't imagine life without you in it. I love you too, and I know we'll be okay."

Soon it was May, the time for my Junior Prom. The dance was semiformal, and Mom and I went shopping for a dress. We found a breathtaking short gown of ecru peau de soie, covered with a delicate gold lace. It was fitted through the waist, and then belled out with a full skirt. It made me feel like a princess.

Our plan for the evening of the prom was to go out to dinner and then on to the dance. When Ken picked me up, he brought me a beautiful wrist corsage of cream-colored roses, and I knew the night would be perfect. Dad, somewhat grudgingly, took pictures of us, and I was sure there was never a happier couple. I felt more beautiful than ever, confident in myself and in Ken's devotion to me. When we walked into the gym, we saw that it had been transformed into a wonderland. At that moment I had no doubt that I had become the young woman I had always dreamed of being.

Dressed up for my junior prom.

Ken's parents were away for the weekend, so when the dance was over, we went to his house. We gave ourselves to each other willingly, yet in our youthful clumsiness, neglected to use protection. It wasn't the first time that had happened, and we berated ourselves for not planning better, resolving to make sure to use it next time.

Ken reassured me. "Greg has been having sex for years and has never gotten anyone pregnant. It's not that easy, sweetheart. Don't worry, I promise to be more careful next time." I went and washed myself carefully, sure this routine would render me safe from pregnancy.

The school year quickly came to an end, and now I was a senior! Soon I would be applying to colleges and making plans for my adult future. I had never been happier. The summer was filled with dates at the stock car races, languid afternoons and evenings drifting or fishing on Ken's boat, and long walks at the reservoir. I resumed my job behind the discount store jewelry counter, and Ken continued to work at the catalog store.

One Saturday afternoon in August, shortly after Ken's twentieth birthday, as we were walking hand in hand through a department store parking lot, we imagined what it would be like when we were married and had a home of our own. I decided to share with him that I had missed three periods. He looked surprised. "Has that ever happened before, honey?" he asked.

"Well," I replied cautiously, "actually it has. I'm never very regular and I have missed several months in a row before."

"Oh, then there's really nothing to worry about, is there?" he said convincingly. "When you get it we'll just have to go out to dinner to celebrate."

"We've been pretty careful," I asserted, "at least lately. I'll let you know when I get it." He hugged me, and we continued planning our future.

CHAPTER 7
Shame

School started again, and Dad really clamped down on me. I had seen so much of Ken over the summer that Dad was barely speaking to me at all. I wanted to spend every spare minute with Ken, but Dad concentrated on making sure I did my schoolwork so I would get into college. My grades weren't outstanding, but they were certainly more than acceptable.

I became vaguer and vaguer about telling my parents my whereabouts during the time I spent away from home. Many afternoons I would sneak over to Ken's house before coming home from school. Dad challenged me and again imposed the limited visitations. I became more defiant. The fights became more frequent.

I missed my old relationship with Dad so much. At night I would hear him and my mother arguing about me. I wanted so badly for our lives to be the way I remembered from my childhood . . . before the fights . . . before I had changed.

Finally, in mid-October, my father had taken as much as he could take. "It's over," he bellowed. "That's it. You are never to see that boy again. You will obey me, and that's all there is to it."

"Daddy, please don't do this. I love him and I love you."

"You'll get over it. You're too young to be tied down to just one person. He's not Jewish. There is no future for the two of you. This isn't right. I won't have it. Tell him you won't see him again!" he demanded.

I cried and begged, but to no avail. My father was adamant. I didn't see any other choice but to tell Ken I couldn't see him anymore. My family was falling apart, and it was my fault. The only thing that would save it would be if I broke up with Ken.

We met one last time, and the pain was excruciating. I explained, "I love you, Kenny, but it has to be this way, at least for now. I have to do the things my father asks of me. Maybe in the future, when we're older, but not now."

We cried as we held each other. How would we make it without one another? I didn't know, but I had no option but to do as my father asked. Several days later I received a letter from Ken. Written in his controlled hand were a poem he had written telling the story of our love, and a letter saying goodbye.

Maybe someday things may change, he wrote, *and we can openly show our love again. No other girl will receive my love until I'm sure that all hope is gone. I'm not going out for a long time, and when I do, it won't be for love, but for friendship. I will never love again as I loved you, and I hope you feel the same way too.*

Please don't do the same things with other guys that we did together. I'll ride up to the reservoir each Sunday afternoon, just to remember, and I'll always think of you when I hear the song, You Belong to Me. If you ever have any trouble with anything, please call me. I'll always be ready to help you with anything you need. Fran, whatever you do, never stop loving me. When you're with someone else, never forget me . . . I'll love you always."

My heart ached, and I cried as I read his words. I raised the envelope to my lips and kissed it, inhaling the scent of the paper and ink as if it would bring him back to me. A panic began to rise in me and I lay down on my bed. I put my hands to my stomach and applied pressure. It was so hard. I was so afraid. I still had not had my period. It was impossible. I couldn't be pregnant. I dismissed the idea. I cried because I couldn't face another day without Ken.

As I came out of school one day the following week, I saw him. As he came toward me I noticed how dejected he looked. "Fran, please, we have to talk," he begged.

"Kenny, don't. I can't do this. Please let's just accept it. Maybe in the future, but not now. I have to do what my father wants." Devastated, he went away.

The following weekend I went to the movies with Ennis. When we left the theater, a light rain was falling. The chilly dampness matched my mood. When we got to my car, I was surprised to find a note under the windshield. I picked it up and studied it by the dashboard light.

Frani, don't worry. I'm not following you; I was just out and saw your car. I don't usually look as bad as when I saw you the other day. It's just been so hard without you. Remember everything we meant to each other. I'll back off for now. I love you.

It was signed in Ken's unmistakable handwriting.

Despite my heartache, things were better at home. Mom and Dad had stopped fighting. Sidra was kinder than usual, and I had lost all my defiance. I was determined to do whatever necessary to win back my father's favor. Then, perhaps later, when I was safely away at college, I could resume my romance with Ken.

My mother was well aware of my depression. "I wish I could help you, honey," she mused. "How about a visit to Edie in New York? You always enjoy spending time with her, don't you? I'm sure Daddy would agree."

I hadn't seen my friend Edie for some time, so Dad encouraged me to visit her at her home in the Bronx. Edie and I had met when we were eight years old at the summer camp my grandparents ran with my aunt and uncle. We had been friends ever since, spending time together every summer and writing each other during the rest of the year. Occasionally my grandparents brought her to Connecticut when they came for a visit from the Bronx, and we caught up with the events in our lives.

Edie seemed so sophisticated compared to me. She was a true "city girl" who knew her way around New York by bus and subway. She went to shows and museums, lived in an apartment, and had been dating for years. Edie had skipped a grade in school, so even though we were the same age, she had already finished high school and was in college.

I was always happy when I was with Edie. She radiated a contagious confidence and warmth. We made arrangements for me to go to my grandparents' home, and from there to Edie's. Despite my grandfather's reservations about Edie's parents being away for the weekend,

Dad agreed. After all, Edie was in college and trustworthy, and I would be far away from Ken. Edie and I planned to shop, go out to eat, and go on a date with her boyfriend Mark and one of his friends. Even though I still missed Ken, I was excited to be doing a "New York thing," and was interested in testing my social confidence on a guy who didn't know me.

Our dates picked us up at Edie's apartment. *Edie Goldberg, Mark Cohen, and Larry Horowitz,* I thought wryly. *All these Jews should make my parents happy.*

We traveled in Larry's car to Coney Island in Brooklyn. It was astonishing—the lights, the boardwalk, Nathan's hot dogs. This was the world my parents had inhabited as teenagers, and I felt a certain bond with them by participating in the kind of thing they had enjoyed, knowing they would approve.

We went back to Edie's place and Larry sat next to me on the sofa. He told me that he'd had a really nice time, and gave me an awkward kiss. When he stepped up his efforts to further the activity, I resisted. His kiss had done nothing for me, and I was not interested in continuing. Larry respected my rebuff, and I was pleased with myself for being able to have a good time without feeling any obligation.

After the boys left, Edie and I talked as we lay in our beds. In the safety of darkness, we poured out our most private thoughts to one another. I told her how much I missed Ken and how lonely I was without him. Then I confessed, "Edie, I'm scared. I haven't had my period since June."

"My God, Fran," she replied, aghast. "Do you think you're pregnant?"

"I don't know…how do you find out? I mean … we were careful most of the time and … but my stomach is so hard … but I couldn't possibly be pregnant … besides, I've always been so irregular. Forget it."

"Fran," she urged me, "the only way to be sure is to see a doctor. Promise me you'll go."

"Edie," I assured her, "I'm positive I'll get it soon. Don't worry . . . I'll let you know as soon as I do."

As I rested on my back, my hands gently pressed my firm abdomen. I felt a fluttering inside, like nothing I had ever felt before.

Is it possible? I thought incredulously. *I can't possibly be pregnant. It couldn't be true, or could it?*

The following week I casually sought out my mother's advice. "Mom, I'm sure with all the stress and everything, it's just not coming. Look, my stomach's so hard, it's going to be a heavy one when it comes."

"Sweetie," she answered easily. "Let me make an appointment with Dr. DeVoe; she's my gynecologist. Perhaps she can give you a shot or something to bring on your period. You're old enough to see that kind of doctor now."

"Sure, Mom." I felt so much better, secure that a simple thing like a shot would be all I needed to help me feel less bloated.

On Saturday morning, November 5, 1963 at nine o'clock, I walked, somewhat nervously, into Dr. DeVoe's office. As instructed, I changed into the garments her assistant left for me and waited in the examination room.

"Good morning, Fran," the kind-looking older woman offered gently. "Your Mom tells me you haven't had your period in a while. Just lie down here and let me take a look at you."

I rested my body on the examining table. She applied her hands firmly to my abdomen and her eyes took on a faraway expression. "You can give me a shot to bring on my period, right?" I said hopefully.

"I need to do an internal examination," she said solemnly. She helped me put my legs into the stirrups and inserted the speculum. It was cold, and my stomach wrenched. She shined a light on my draped internal organs. I felt a mild pinching, and she was done. "Get dressed dear, and come into my office."

I did as I was told. As I walked over to the chair across from her desk and slowly sat down, a chill came over me.

"Fran," she began. "It appears that you are about five months pregnant."

"I can't be pregnant. I can't, I can't, it's just not true," I protested.

"I'm afraid there's no doubt. Based on the dates you've told me, and from the appearance of your cervix, I'd say you are due about the seventeenth of March." My whole body went numb. I could not think and I could not move.

"Fran," she stated, "I want you to go directly home and tell your mother. I will call your house at eleven o'clock, and if you have not told her by then, I will tell her myself."

Somehow, I found my way home. I walked into the house and ran to my mother's arms.

"What is it . . . oh my God, no, oh, no!" she cried.

"Mommy, I'm sorry. I'm so sorry," I wept.

"I have to call your father to come home from the office."

She ran to the phone. I sat rigidly in a kitchen chair, nauseated and terrified. The half hour between the phone call and the time my father arrived home was interminable. My fear of my father's wrath was profound. I was so ashamed. I had tried so hard to save the family by doing his bidding and breaking up with Ken, but it was too late. I had already ruined the family forever.

A short time later, my father walked heavily into the house. We moved into the living room and I sat down in one of the club chairs. He stood over me as I cowered.

"Oh, Fran, my God," he said, choking back tears. I began weeping uncontrollably. Sidra sat silently, cowering in another chair. My mother sat pale faced and trembling on the sofa.

Dad spoke again. "Who knows about this?" he asked sternly.

"Nobody . . . nobody," I replied, stammering.

"Are you sure? Think!" he yelled.

"Well," I attempted, "I told Edie I was late, but I was sure I couldn't be . . . "

"Fran, Fran," he went on, "how could you do this? Who else, who else did you tell?"

"Wh . . . when I was first late I told Kenny, but we never talked about it again . . . he doesn't know . . . I should call him."

"NO, absolutely NOT!" my father roared. "You will NEVER talk with him again . . . he is NOT to know anything about this!"

I became hysterical. I was so humiliated, ashamed, powerless, such a failure.

"I want to die, oh God, I want to die," I screamed. I wanted to disappear.

My father became even angrier. "Control yourself, Fran. Get some self-control! Anita, get her a Valium or something. Fran, STOP IT NOW!" I tried to catch my breath, but my sobs would not abate.

My mother brought me a pill and a glass of water. "Here," she said dispassionately, "take this. It will calm you down." I did as I was told.

"Your mother and I need time to think, to discuss this. Go to your room. You are not to use the telephone, do you understand?" "Yes," I said, choking on the lump in my throat. I went to my room and waited. The events of the rest of the afternoon were a blur. The drug worked well . . . I heard the sound of animated conversation between my parents as if I was underwater, punctuated by my father's deep moans.

The next evening, we went to the home of my father's sister, my Aunt Ethel. She knew from the look on my father's face that something was very wrong. Her young children, my cousins, were sent from the room, and her husband busied himself in another part of the house.

I silently found a corner of the sofa in which to disappear. My father took a breath and uttered barely audibly, "She's pregnant."

My beloved aunt looked at me, pained. I wanted to run to her and have her insulate me from it all, but I could not move.

"What can I do to help?" she asked.

My father replied. "She's too far along for an abortion—even if it were legal in Connecticut, which it isn't. We thought of Puerto Rico, but the doctor said no one will do abortions in the fifth month."

Thank God, I thought. *I don't want an abortion. I love Kenny and I love our baby.*

But Dad had it all worked out. He devised a story to save our family from disgrace. Purportedly, my parents and I had a terrible fight over my resistance to breaking up with Ken. They would tell people that I threatened to run away with Ken or kill myself. Naturally, my father would never allow that to happen, so he made arrangements to have me go away. I would then be gone from Ken's influence, and would learn that my father's word was law. Since I was always such a nice girl, no one would ever believe anything else. And because my father's strictness was the norm, his decision, though severe, made the story believable.

My mother's parents, Grandpa Irving and Grandma Ceil, were to play a crucial role in the plan. Grandpa, at age sixty-seven, agreed to retire from his job. Grandma, only sixty-three, was anxious to get out of the Bronx. She had recently been mugged on the sidewalk outside her apartment, and was willing and eager to leave New York for the winter. It was arranged that they would take me away with them and make sure that by the time spring came, the baby would have been born and I would have forgotten about Ken. Besides Aunt Ethel, Grandpa Irving, Grandma Ceil, Sidra and my parents, no one was to ever know the truth. My mother's brother, Uncle Jay and his wife Aunt Lee would be told "the story," as would my paternal grandparents, Grandpa Abe and Grandma Esther.

Look what I've done, I thought. *My sin is so shameful that my parents can't even share the truth with their closest family.*

Aunt Ethel became my "babysitter" for the next two weeks. Whenever my mother had to be away from the house, Aunt Ethel was there to make sure I didn't attempt to call Ken or any of my other friends. Mom and Dad instructed me to write Edie and tell her that the doctor had given me a shot to bring on my period . . . that the whole thing had been a false alarm.

Dad selected Tucson, Arizona as our destination because it was a place where we would be extremely unlikely to meet anyone we knew. He designed an itinerary for our trip that included tourist attractions from Washington, DC to Los Angeles, California. We planned to stop in Tucson for the coldest part of the winter, and that was where I would give birth. Dad instructed us to take photographs along the way that showed us having a grand time—photographs that showed my supposedly "unpregnant" figure. This part was easy because I was young and thin, and my pregnancy did not show at all.

All transactions would be done in cash at doctors' offices and hospitals as well as for our apartment rental, so there would be no paper trail. My grandparents would have a post office box as a mailing address in Tucson so there would be no surprise visits from anyone. All my mail, both to and from my friends, was to be routed through my parents. They screened my correspondence and forwarded the letters so there would be no way that anyone could tell Ken where I was.

After I had the baby, I was to give it up for adoption. Only then could we return home. By April I could go back to being the obedient, nice daughter everyone believed me to be.

Once the plan was made, Mom went to my school to withdraw me. She used the story that she and Dad had invented about my rebelliousness.

My guidance counselor grumbled that my father certainly was strict, but of course he knew what was best. My mother assured him I would return to school as soon as my defiant behavior ceased.

I spent the following weekend in my grandparents' New York apartment. It was too much of a risk for me to be home where someone they didn't want me to see might drop by.

I faced my adored Grandma Ceil—she reached for me and held me in her arms, and rocked me. "Oh my *shana maidel*," she said, as she tried to comfort me with Yiddish words of affection. I wanted her to hold me and rock me forever. I felt so safe next to her bosom. But my eyes could not meet Grandpa Irving's. He never said a word to me about what I had done, but I could tell from his demeanor how disappointed he was with me.

I helped them pack up their apartment for the winter, and returned home to Connecticut on Sunday evening to begin packing my own belongings for our trip.

We were scheduled to leave the following Saturday. Late that week, my mother got a distressing phone call. Uncle Jay, only thirty-five years old, was in the hospital. He had suffered a mild heart attack. Along with Grandpa Irving and Grandma Ceil, Mom rushed to New York to be with him. The damage was not serious, but Uncle Jay would have to remain in the hospital for several weeks. My parents and grandparents conferred about what to do. Satisfied that Uncle Jay would be okay, they decided to go ahead with the trip as scheduled.

It was imperative they get me out of town as quickly as possible. Despite his health scare, Uncle Jay was not told the true story behind our trip. The anger, disillusionment, and hurt my uncle felt at his parents' abandonment during his illness rested on my shoulders. The rift between them over this was not to be healed for more than twenty years.

We departed on Saturday, November 19 as planned. We drove south through Washington, DC, Virginia, the Carolinas, and Georgia, and then west to Alabama. On Tuesday, November 22, we stopped for lunch in Montgomery. The restaurant patrons were all abuzz with the news that President Kennedy had been shot while in a motorcade in Dallas. My heart broke as I joined the millions of others across the nation who feared the worst about the fate of their president. The knowledge that this day would be forever embedded in the psyche of my entire generation had yet to sink in.

"Where were you when President Kennedy was assassinated?" Over the years that followed, I heard this question scores of times. My peers were in school. They cried and comforted one another, trying to make sense of the greatest tragedy of our generation. I, however, was in a restaurant in Montgomery, Alabama. I was a thousand miles from my home, my friends, my life . . . pregnant with the child of my lost love.

I was feeling lonely and depressed as we spent Thanksgiving on the road. I believed I had little for which to be thankful. We drove across Texas and New Mexico, and finally arrived in Tucson. We were lucky to find a clean and friendly one bedroom garden apartment near the University of Arizona. The units all opened to a central courtyard that contained a swimming pool. Occupied primarily by retirees and a few students, it was quiet and private. Grandma and Grandpa took the bedroom, and I slept on the convertible sofa in the living room. It was small, but adequate for our short stay.

Tucson was so unlike home. The terrain was flat, and one could see for miles in every direction. The horizon was filled with the broad expanse of snow-capped Mount Lemmon. Palm trees lined the wide avenues. The days in the desert were warm and dry. Here I could pull up a lounge chair next to the pool with a book, and lose myself for a while.

Outside our motel in New Orleans, November 1963.

Of course the story we used in Tucson was different. Since my pregnancy was to become obvious soon, I was transformed into an impulsive young woman who had secretly eloped with her boyfriend to Maryland. Soon after our marriage, he had joined the army and was sent abroad. When my enraged parents found out what I had done, they'd had the marriage annulled. After all that, I had discovered I was pregnant.

The only solution was to give this child to a family who could not have one. I almost came to believe this myth myself. The neighbors never talked with me about my situation. My grandparents had obviously done a good job telling them how sensitive I was about it all. I began to feel quite noble and proud of the

Grandpa Irving and Grandma Ceil. On our way to Tucson, December 1963.

good deed I was about to do for a family that could not exist were it not for my benevolent act.

I transformed myself into the vessel that carried another woman's child. I had no rights to this child, no claim on its future. My only responsibility was to see that I remained healthy and carried it to term. At night, resting in bed, I manipulated its little arms and legs, felt it moving, and marveled at the life growing inside me.

The changes in my body sometimes frightened me. No one explained to me what was happening or what would happen. I had heard stories of the pain of childbirth, but had no idea if or how that might apply to me. I could not bring myself to ask. I didn't want to cause anyone any trouble. I decided I would have to wait and see.

Sometimes I imagined that Ken would find out where I was and gallantly come and rescue me. Then I felt guilty at the idea of disappointing my family once again. I went back to believing that my life was temporarily off track, and that my redemption was to do a good deed for another family. I even thought that someday, when I married, I would have two biological children, then adopt another. Somehow, that would even the score.

Once I go home, I thought, *I'll be perfect. I'll do everything Daddy wants me to do. I'll get good grades, go to a good college, then I'll be an adult. Kenny and I will get back together. We'll get married and find our baby.* It all seemed so logical. It was fantasies like these that held me together.

None of us expected the entrance of another young man into my life. Mal lived several doors down from us. Friendly and well mannered, studious and independent, he was in graduate school studying business. Best of all, he won the stamp of approval for being Jewish.

We soon began to talk regularly. I told the Arizona version of the story for the first time myself. He accepted it without too many questions, being more interested in me as a person. We spent time together reading, watching TV, playing cards, and smoking cigarettes. It was nice to have someone close to my own age to talk to. He was in his early twenties and was aware that I was only seventeen, but he treated me as if I were as mature as he.

His family lived in Scottsdale, an affluent suburb of Phoenix, where his father was in the garment business. When Mal finished his degree, he planned to go to New York and participate in the family business from there. My grandparents believed he would be a good influence on me, and encouraged our friendship.

CHAPTER 8
Arizona

*T*ime passed quickly in Tucson. Every day we did something different. We went to museums, a rodeo, and missions. We visited the desert as well as tourist traps like Old Tucson. We took a day trip to Nogales, Mexico where we were gripped by the liveliness and obvious poverty of the community. We drove up to the snow line on Mount Lemmon where I pretended, if only for a moment, that we were close to my New England home. We visited department stores to buy accessories and a few new things to accommodate the small but persistent widening of my waistline. We bought Mexican and Native American gifts and souvenirs. I purchased a traditional serape blanket in colors of maroon, blue, red, and gold. In a Native American shop I treated myself to a gold velvet pullover blouse with silver concha buttons and to a silver thunderbird charm for my charm bracelet.

Soon after our arrival in Tucson, we contacted a physician whom Dr. DeVoe had recommended. She had picked his name out of a book, looked at his credentials, and believed he would be acceptable. She had given me my records to take with me, and I presented the new obstetrician with the folder of Joan Gross, the name I was to use in every record or document during my preg-

Grandma Ceil and me at Old Tucson, January 1964.

nancy. How this name came to be, I will never know. My mother preferred to remember it as a clerical error. I believe it was my father's contrivance. I accepted my pseudonym without dissent—I did what I was told.

Dr. Janssen was a tall thin man in his forties. He did not ask too many questions, nor did he give much advice. Grandma would come into the examination room with me, and he would nod and say that everything was coming along just fine. It was understood that I would be giving this baby up, and he said he would take care of the details.

One day in January we were driving to the market. I was sitting in the front seat with Grandpa. A car in front of us stopped short, and Grandpa slammed on the brakes. The inertia threw my body forward, and I found myself lying in a breathless heap on the floor of the car.

"Fran, are you hurt?" Grandma cried from her seat in the back.

I examined myself and called out, "I think so . . . oh, my head, I bumped my head." A lump had formed on my forehead, and I was alarmed. I pulled myself up and regained my composure.

"We better take you to see Dr. Janssen," Grandpa cautioned. "We need to be sure everything is all right."

Dr. Janssen agreed to see me right away. He examined me closely and verified that everything was okay. The baby had not been compromised in any way by the accident, but Dr. Janssen told me to have Grandpa quit smoking his smelly cigars around me! The next day, Grandpa had seat belts installed in his car.

This was the winter of 1964, which was marked by the arrival of the Beatles in America. With them came the beginning not only of a revolution in music, but a revolution in attitudes and mores as well. My peers and those younger than I may have enjoyed the new-found freedoms that the cultural transformations of the times brought, but my unique experience kept me isolated and impervious to these changes.

By February I didn't feel like going out much anymore. I was aware of my pregnancy being pretty obvious to anyone who gave me more than a cursory glance, and I was sure my youthful face belied the story I told. However, one day Grandma convinced me to go to Steinfeld's, a large department store—just to get out of the apartment. I put on a coat, ostensibly to keep out the mild winter chill, but more to hide my rotund shape. As we strolled through the store, I became warmer and warmer. Suddenly I found that not only was I warm, I was extremely dizzy. The world began spinning and I couldn't focus my eyes. For the first time in my life, I fainted. A trip to Dr. Janssen revealed no organic cause for my collapse.

"Perhaps you just need to take it easy, get plenty of fresh air, and rest until your time comes," he suggested.

So I spent the balance of my days sitting by the pool reading or chatting with Mal, feeling terribly isolated and sorry for myself. The days dragged on and on, interminably.

Early in the morning on March 7, I woke in the darkness to pain in my abdomen. I lay very still, thinking that if I didn't move, the tightness would go away. It did not. *It's not March 17 yet,* I thought. As the dawn broke, I called out to Grandma. "I think it's time for me to go to the hospital." We hurried to leave and drove quickly to the hospital in the early morning light.

I remember little else about that chaotic time—it was as if I weren't there. Hushed voices, bodies moving efficiently about their business . . . then waking in a private room. Grandma was standing next to me quietly calling my name. "Fran, Fran, can you hear me?" she murmured.

"Yes," I replied weakly. The glare from the sun hurt my eyes. Grandpa walked silently over to my bedside and kissed me on the forehead.

"Look who's here to see you, honey," Grandma proclaimed. I looked toward the door. Mal was standing there with a huge bouquet of roses.

"How are you doing, Frani?" Mal asked.

Then I remembered. My hands flew to my stomach. What had been round, firm, and ripe was now flat, soft and barren. Where I had felt movement and vitality, there was now stillness. Where there had been tiny arms and legs to play with, there was nothing. I was physically and emotionally exhausted, and my body felt like I had been hit by a truck.

Was it a boy or a girl? I wondered silently. To Mal I replied, "I'm okay, I guess, but I'm awfully tired."

"Just let me leave these with you," he said. "I'll come back later, I promise." Mal said softly.

After Mal left, Grandpa Irving spoke. "Let's call your mother and father and let them know." He picked up the phone and dialed. "Anita," he said when my mother answered, "It's all over." There was quiet, and then he said, "She's fine; I'll put her on."

My mother asked how I was feeling and I told her how tired I was. "Soon you'll be coming home," she offered. "You can get back to living your life."

"Yeah, soon, Mommy," I replied, handing the phone to Grandma Ceil. My thoughts raced. *Did I really have a baby? No one has said a word about a baby. There are no babies here. Was it all a dream?*

After Grandma and Grandpa left, a nurse came into the room. She smiled a polite little half-smile and told me she was here to check me.

She pressed down so hard on my stomach it took my breath away. Without comment, she changed my pad and told me I would have to get up soon to use the bathroom. "Sit up, Joan," she ordered. "I have to wrap you."

Joan, I thought. Then I remembered. Here I was Joan Gross—for the records, of course.

"Wrap me?" I queried. She loosened my hospital gown, took a wide swath of cloth and began winding it around me, mummy style, to bind my breasts.

"This is so your milk won't come in. I'm going to give you a shot, too." I didn't understand, but I was too embarrassed to ask any questions. She

Postpartum. Outside our apartment in Tucson, March 1964.

certainly knew I was an unwed mother, but made no mention of my baby.

My baby. What about my baby? I was mute. I had no right to ask any questions; I only had to be obedient.

Two days later it became obvious that all the wrapping and the shot had done no good. I awoke soaked with the milk that oozed from my breasts. My body knew that I had given birth, even if no one else had acknowledged that fact.

In a few more days I was discharged from the hospital. I

continued to sleep at night with my hands pressed to my stomach—waiting, hoping to feel something. There was nothing.

The following weekend, Mal invited me to go to Scottsdale for the weekend to meet his family. Grandma and Grandpa conferred with my parents. "It will do her good to get away for a couple of days. He's a nice young man, a gentleman, and his family is anxious to meet her," Grandpa urged.

They consented to let me go. How much risk was there in allowing a zombie, still bleeding after childbirth, to go anywhere with a nice young gentleman? Sitting in Mal's convertible, flying across the desert, I felt almost normal again. My hair blew in the hot wind, and I was going to a new destination, finally liberated from constant observation and concern. When we arrived at his home, I gingerly and slowly exited the car. I was still a little sore, but I could walk without that being obvious if I took it easy.

Mal introduced me to his mother, father, and younger sister. His sister was almost my age, and scrutinized me for quite a while, politely saying hello. His parents were warm and gracious. I speculated as to whether or not he had told them anything about me, and figured that he certainly hadn't told them I'd had a baby the week before! I was sure they would have been shocked.

His mother prepared a wonderful dinner, and while we ate, we talked about what it was like back east, and his parents' childhoods spent in New York. Afterward, Mal and I went for a walk down the street. When we returned, his family had gone their various ways, leaving us alone in the TV room. We sat and watched the screen, talking for some time about nothing in particular. As I rose to say goodnight and go to the guest room, Mal caught my hand and pulled me to him, kissing me lightly on the lips. I was so startled I pulled back.

"Fran," he declared. "I love you. I've been wanting to tell you for such a long time, but I couldn't while you were . . . well, now you're . . . now it's okay to tell you how I feel." Apprehension slowly gripped my chest. What could I say to him? I felt NOTHING. I was empty. I had nothing to give, and I wanted no part of a romantic relationship with anyone. Mal was sweet, but I felt only friendship for him. I was still bound to Ken, to the core of my soul. I finally gained enough composure to speak. "Mal,

I'm so surprised," I told him. "I'm truly flattered that you feel that way about me . . . but . . . but I'm not ready for a relationship with anyone yet . . . it's too soon."

"I understand," he said soberly. "I just had to tell you how I feel. You are so special, and you mean so much to me."

"I care for you, Mal. I do, but I can't have feelings like that for anyone right now. It's just not in me."

"It's okay," he said, kissing me fleetingly on the head. "I'll see you in the morning." The next day was spent souvenir shopping and seeing the sights of Phoenix, before we made the trip back to Tucson. Mal indeed was a gentleman, and did not press the issue of his feelings for me.

The week went quickly, and on Saturday, March 21, Grandma Ceil and I visited the office of a social worker. I sat in a chair facing her. The woman sat at her desk, and a huge window behind her had the venetian blinds drawn in such a way that sunlight was sprayed in zebra stripes all over her office. The glare of the light was distracting, and it was hard to focus on her face. While she spoke, Grandma sat quietly behind me on the sofa.

"Now, Joan," the social worker began. "Let's see. Your eyes are blue, hair brown, height?"

"Five-six," I supplied.

"Weight?" she continued.

Now or before, I wondered. I guessed somewhere in between. "Uh . . . one twenty?"

"Your interests, talents," she probed.

I tried to form my words carefully. Lost in reverie . . . I replied, "I like to read, play the piano, take walks (*in the woods by the reservoir with Ken,* I remembered), go to the movies."

"Education?" she queried.

"I've finished eleventh grade. After I graduate I'm going to college to be a teacher," I added hopefully.

"Thank you dear. Now tell me about the father."

"W . . . What?" I stammered.

"What does he look like?" she urged.

How could I begin to describe him? The feelings came rushing back, and my heart began to beat furiously. *Oh Kenny . . . where are you? I need you. Don't let this happen.*

"He's six feet tall, brown hair, brown eyes, about one hundred seventy pounds," I offered. I couldn't tell her about the tiny dimple in his left cheek when he smiled, or the soft sound of his voice, or the ways his arms had held me.

"Religion?" she asked.

"Lutheran," I replied.

"Do you care what religion the baby is raised in?" she inquired.

I thought for a moment. *If Ken and I were the same religion we might be married now.* The difference in our religions had been responsible for separating us . . . I didn't want my child's chances of finding a loving family to be limited by religion.

"No," I answered without looking at Grandma. "I don't care."

"Hobbies, talents, education?" she persisted.

I closed my eyes and pictured his lithe frame shooting basketballs, throwing a bowling ball, his strong hands shifting gears in the car where I sat next to him. "He's very athletic," I said. "He's a junior in college, studying to become a math teacher."

"Umm . . . " she muttered.

"Excuse me?" I asked.

"His name . . . I need his name," she repeated.

My panic rose higher. I was not prepared for this question.

"Does it matter . . . his name?" I had to think fast. I was not even using my own name; I had to protect Ken, too.

"Yes, dear, we must have his name for our records."

"Kenny . . . Kenneth," slipped from my lips. I hadn't spoken his name in so long. I had to think of something fast. *What could I do to Jamison?*

"James," I said. "Kenneth James."

"Now sign here, dear," she said. "This is the relinquishment paper. After this you'll never have to think about any of this again."

My eyes filled with tears. Never think of this again? How could that ever be possible? My head was pounding, my heart was beating wildly, and I was extremely nauseated. With barely a glance at the document in front of me, I took the pen that she handed me. Shaking, I carefully wrote the alien name, Joan Gross.

CHAPTER 9
Eighteen

The following Monday we said good-bye to Mal and the other neighbors, packed our things and left Tucson. I gave Mal my home address, and he said he would stay in touch. Per Dad's instructions, we were to continue our "vacation" and head west to California.

With some excitement we entered Los Angeles and made plans to visit all the tourist attractions. We enjoyed seeing the sights in Hollywood—the Wax Museum, Grauman's Chinese Theater, and the Walk of the Stars. We toured Knott's Berry Farm, ate at the Brown Derby Restaurant, and of course spent a day at Disneyland.

At my father's behest we spent an afternoon with his cousin Sonny and his family. They were thrilled to meet us and told us stories of the good times they had shared with Dad when they were growing up in New York. Sonny had a son a few years older than I, and he entertained me with tales of his life in L.A.

I know Dad had spoken with them prior to our arrival, but I was not aware if they had been told "the story." I assumed they had. Blessedly, they did not say anything to me about my personal life. However, I was sure they would be reporting back to other family members precisely how I looked. We took lots of pictures of a slender me to add to the collection of images of me in tight pants, shorts and bathing suits that we had already sent back to my parents.

Despite the allure of southern California, the three of us were extremely anxious to go home. Winter was over, as was our mission. We all wanted to resume a more normal life. We were determined to make the trip east as quickly as possible, and planned minimal sightseeing on the way.

After some quick stops at Hoover Dam, Las Vegas, the Petrified Forest, and Meteor Crater, we arrived at the Grand Canyon on Monday, April 6, my eighteenth birthday.

The day was cold and gray. Snowflakes sputtered from the sky. I went to the posted viewing area and surveyed the expanse before me. There was nothing I'd ever seen that compared. The canyon was so huge, it didn't look real. It went on and on forever. Yet, as I looked out over the vast emptiness in front of me, I could only think of the vast emptiness I felt inside myself. There was no running away from the void, the nothingness of my soul. I missed my baby; I missed Ken; I missed the love and respect of my parents; I missed the happy young girl I had been a year before. Now, it was all forever lost to me. On my eighteenth birthday I felt as if my life had no purpose.

By mid-April, we arrived home. Dad arranged for construction to begin on an in-law apartment attached to our house, which would accommodate Grandma Ceil and Grandpa Irving. When the addition was completed, they would move permanently out of their place in New York, come to live with us for most of the year, and spend their winters in Florida.

Mom took me back to the gynecologist to make sure I was healthy. She urged the physician to give me birth control pills to regulate my period. I suppose that was her way of telling herself it wouldn't happen again, while giving me the reasoning that my irregular cycle needed to be adjusted.

I signed up to take secretarial courses in shorthand and typing at a nearby business school. That would keep me busy for the rest of the spring, and I'd learn something productive as well. I decided then that I would really show everyone how competent I could be. I did classwork and homework in those two courses as if my life depended on it. In many ways, I guess it did. I felt driven to prove my value, and to earn the approval of the adults in my life. By June, I had worked my way up to typing an impressive eighty words a minute. My teachers were astounded, and I think my parents were, too.

CHAPTER 10
Building a New Fran

For the summer, my father got me a job working in his cousin's law office. It was quiet; I could use my new secretarial skills, and I would be out of the public eye.

In dribs and drabs, a few of my friends dared to call and visit me. I was terrified at each reunion. It was embarrassing for me to be with them since they had graduated and I had not. The Class of '64 ring I had worn so proudly the year before now had no meaning. It sat unworn in my jewelry box. One or the other of my parents was never far away. There was nothing I could do without permission. My phone calls continued to be screened and my visitors monitored. My social life outside the house was nonexistent.

Dad explained his reasoning to me. "Since you showed us that you didn't know how to make the right decisions, we'll have to remake you from the beginning. You'll learn from scratch what is expected of you, and you will gradually learn to follow the right path. We'll start from the beginning, like we did when you were an infant, and teach you again."

I learned that in my parents' eyes, I was nothing; I was incapable of making any kind of decision on my own. If I didn't do it Dad's way, I didn't do it. His motto was: "if you have a decision to make, always think of what I would say about it. If you can't decide, then don't do it." He always made sense. It was easy to believe him because he was so incredibly sure of himself.

My father was not a bad man. He was trying to raise me and my sister the way he had been raised. It had worked for him, and he assumed it would work with his children. We had never, ever been disciplined physically, but what worked best for Dad was the withholding of affection. He truly believed what he was doing was right.

It wasn't long before I received a letter from Mal. He had finished school and was coming to New York to explore the job possibilities, just as he'd always dreamed he would. He wanted to see me, to meet my family, and renew our friendship.

I showed the letter to my father. He thought for a minute, then spoke. "I think this is a good idea. It's important, however, for you to tell Mal that no one here knows what happened, and that we would appreciate it if he didn't mention it to anyone."

I agreed. "Of course, Daddy. There's nothing to worry about. I'll write Mal and tell him." I had no doubt about Mal's discretion.

And so, Mal came to visit. He was delighted to see me. Grandma and Grandpa greeted him enthusiastically, and my parents were welcoming and hospitable to him. With some trepidation, I introduced him to Grandpa Abe and Grandma Esther, hoping that their meeting him in person would dispel any doubts they had about the veracity of the story behind my trip.

Mal and I spent little time alone. I knew he still cared for me in a way I was unprepared to reciprocate. So, I kept things light and amicable, totally platonic, between us. When the weekend was over, it was clear that Mal had gotten the message. I was back home in the cradle of my family, sheltered and unavailable to him.

We agreed to write, but I knew that I wouldn't have to worry about him pressuring me into a relationship in which I had no interest.

In spite of being busy all summer, I thought constantly about what I had been through. I was forever changed, and wondered incessantly what had become of the baby I had never seen and never held. One day, I bravely approached my mother. "Mommy, do you know if I had a boy or a girl?"

She looked enormously uncomfortable, took a deep breath, and

With my sister Sidra, August 1964.

softly answered. "Sweetheart, no one ever told me. Daddy and I were think-ing if it were a boy there would have been a notation on the hospital bill with a charge for circumcision. There wasn't one, so I guess it was a girl."

I wondered incredulously how it was she had managed to avoid asking these questions herself. Was Dad discouraging her from thinking, from feeling? Did he tell her, as he had told me, self-control was the most im-portant thing, and we should get on with our lives as if nothing had hap-pened?

Since Mom displayed such obvious discomfort with the discussion, I realized I wouldn't be able to go to her with my feelings, and was expect-ed to do what I was told to do, simply forget about it and move on. Oh, how hard I tried . . .

When September came, it was time to go back to school. I would re-turn to the same high school and pick up where I left off. I signed up for the same courses, the same extra-curricular activities. If my teachers wondered about my disappearance and reemergence, they said nothing to me about it.

The hardest part about returning to school was making new friends. Most of my friends had graduated and moved on to college or jobs. Even though I was older, I was still expected to participate in the world of high school. I felt ancient on the inside, but I couldn't let that show on the out-side. I was determined to redeem myself in my parents' eyes by showing the world that I was a nice girl, a smart girl, an obedient girl.

Little by little I was permitted to participate socially with my peers. Since Mom was off work on Fridays, on that day I could take the car to school. I could go to the movies, to school functions, or out to eat as long as I followed the rules. I could sometimes almost forget the past.

One Friday night I went with my friend Amy to a basketball game at the high school. One of the players on the team held lots of records and was being scouted by the pros. The whole town came out to see him play. The gym was packed with fans. We yelled and cheered enthusiastically, and were invigorated by the exhilaration of the crowd. At halftime we went from the bleachers to the floor to chat with some friends. As we were making our way back up, I looked into the stands.

There in the top row was Ken. He was sitting quietly and talking to a girl with short brown hair—obviously a date. I felt as if I had been punched. My heart started to beat wildly, and I sensed the familiar panic rising from my stomach. I had to get out. He hadn't seen me . . . I had to leave the gym . . . I couldn't be in the same room with him; I couldn't face him; I was terrified.

"Amy, we have to leave NOW," I insisted.

"Why? Fran, what's wrong?" she inquired, concerned. I could barely speak, but she needed an answer.

"I just . . . we just . . . have to get out of here . . . I don't feel well, I have to go home . . . " I said, gasping for breath.

The fresh air and encouragement from Amy helped me to calm down. It was a short drive to drop her off at her house, and somehow I managed to get myself home. I pulled the car into the garage, put my head down on the steering wheel, and began to cry forlornly.

I have to get control of myself, I thought. *Daddy would be furious if he knew . . . this is not what is expected of me . . . I have to put the past away, . . . but . . . but . . . oh, Kenny, I am so sorry . . .*

School kept me busy enough that I didn't have a lot of time to think about myself. I did my homework with fervor. I was always the first to volunteer an answer in class. I became a model student, a model daughter.

Soon, the time came to make college applications. Mom and Dad had always wanted me to have the experience of going away to school, and decided that since I had been such a conscientious student, they would allow me to do that. They also believed I would certainly be able, by the following fall, to make informed, wise decisions.

I received a minimal amount of assistance from my guidance counselor. Since I had left school, I always felt he viewed me with a bit of skepticism. It may have been my own self-conscious worry, or, perhaps, he had never actually believed the story my family had told about my absence. He suggested I would fit best at a small women's liberal arts college, but I disagreed. That would have been far too intimate for me—I needed to get lost in the crowd and not be too noticeable. I finally decided to apply to three large schools—the University of Connecticut, Syracuse University, and Boston University. Carefully and deliberately, I filled out the required forms, and secured glowing recommendations from my teachers.

After I submitted the applications, one of the schools wrote me and requested more information. The admissions department wanted to know what had happened in the year I was not in school. I thought about it and wrote an exciting report about the "wonderful opportunity" I had been given to travel and see the United States. I had visited more than twenty-six states and believed my extensive travel taught me things I never could have learned in a classroom. While all that was true, I still felt dishonest, leaving out the most important lesson of all.

Spring came, and with it the fat letters of acceptance from all three schools. UCONN was too filled with memories and too close to home. Syracuse was bitter cold and five hours away. So, I decided on Boston University. It was a respectable three hours from home—far enough to offer me a measure of independence, and close enough so I could come home without much effort or expense. The best thing about it was its enormous size—I could reinvent myself there and become the person I wanted to be.

I knew three people from my home town at BU. One was a boy from my graduating class who was studying engineering. Another was my old friend Ronnie Stein. I had seen him only a few times since my return from Arizona, and I believed he was embarrassed at having been the catalyst in my relationship with Ken. He and I had been such good friends before that, and I had truly felt the loss of his friendship. His mother was none too keen on having him hang out with me after she'd heard the rumors that had circulated after my departure.

The third person I knew at BU was Paul. He was two years older than I and we had been members of the same Jewish youth group, so we had some mutual friends.

But college was still several months away, and I threw myself into enjoying what remained of my high school career. I received straight A's that senior year in high school, and in May of 1965 I was inducted into the National Honor Society. The night of my induction was a special one. The students who were to be honored sat on the auditorium stage and were congratulated by school administrators for their hard work and commitment to the school and the community. Our families were all invited to the ceremony that concluded with a dessert reception.

Both sets of my grandparents came to shower me with well wishes, and of course my parents were there. My father, however, was angry with me about something and never said a word to me the entire evening. I can't remember or even imagine what I could have done to upset him so much, especially since I knew my behavior had been close to perfect for the whole year! But, nevertheless, angry he was, and his emotional distance hurt more than any physical pain he could have inflicted.

Prom time came. That entire school year, I had never gone out on a single date. My parents' new rule was that I could not go out with any boy who was not Jewish. That eliminated nearly everyone I knew, but that was okay with me. I didn't much want to deal with boys or feelings anyway. Sidra, now fourteen and seriously interested in boys herself,

Ready for my senior prom, June 1965.

was not thrilled with the tightening of the social laws, and I'm sure she resented me tremendously for it.

Mom had a workable idea. Aunt Lee had a sister whose son was several months older than I. He was nice looking, amiable, and best of all, agreeable to being my date for the prom. I'd known Lenny since we were six years old, and had seen him on and off for many years at family functions. I felt comfortable enough with him to see to it we would both have an enjoyable time. I arranged for us to double date with my old friends Rina and Cal, and was enthusiastically looking forward to prom night.

My gown was long, made of white satin, and had a lace bodice and a long pink bow that tied at the waist. It made me feel regal, pretty, and sweet. It was the perfect dress for a "nice" girl.

Lenny brought me pink sweetheart roses to wear at my wrist, and he looked charming in his tuxedo. My friends were envious of me with such a handsome date. Dad took lots of pictures, and after Cal picked us up, we celebrated at the prom and post-prom party just like all the others.

That was certainly what I wanted most . . . to be just like all the other kids. Somehow, though, the magic was just not there for me. I had a pleasant time, but seeing couples who were in love, like my friends Donna and Bob, brought me back to the time two years earlier when I had been part of a couple in love, and I knew the difference. Ken was the one who was supposed to take me to my senior prom—that was what we had planned. Now it was the wrong year, the wrong prom, the wrong young man.

Graduation went by in a blur. I received a special award from my Social Studies teacher as the best student in her course, "Problems of American Democracy." She encouraged me to pursue my lifelong dream of becoming a teacher, and told me my hard work, intelligence and maturity would be an asset in the classroom.

That summer I worked in the law office again, once more away from the public, away from old friends, and under the watchful eye of Dad's cousin. I was now nineteen years old, but felt as if I were twelve. As competent in school and work as I was, I still believed I would never measure up to my parents' expectations.

CHAPTER 11

A College Girl

*T*he car was stuffed with all my clothes, the new stereo Mom and Dad gave me for graduation, my electric typewriter, and almost everything else I owned. As we sped along the highway toward Boston, I was eagerly anticipating the beginning of the next chapter of my life. I hadn't received word of a roommate assignment, and was nervous about what she would be like. We peered into every passing car, as if every single one of them was on its way to Boston University, too. Mom and Dad joked for three hours, "There's your roommate, Fran!"

We pulled up to the four story brownstone on Buswell Street that was to become my home. I had been assigned to the front suite on the fourth floor, and we lugged my possessions up crooked, narrow stairs. The suite contained four bedrooms—a triple, a double, and a single. I had the single. As I stood, somewhat disappointed in my new little room, Mom put away my clothes and Dad set up my stereo. A cheerful woman with a syrupy Southern drawl stuck her head in the room. She called over her shoulder. "Na-an, Na-ancy, come on over here!" Following her command, a lovely round faced girl with beautiful long blonde hair entered the doorway.

"Hi," she introduced herself. "I'm Nancy."

"Oh, hi, I'm Fran," I offered nervously.

"I'm just across the hall in the triple," she added. "I'm from New Jersey. The other girls are from Massachusetts and New York."

Somehow, in the space of two minutes, my mother had deduced that Nancy and her mother were Jewish. She began chatting with Nancy's mother about all the things mothers somehow find to talk about. I was extremely tense, and awkwardly tried to make conversation.

"Where in New Jersey are you from?" I asked.

"West Orange, you know it?" she replied.

"No, I don't, I'm sorry. We're from Connecticut. Do you belong to any youth groups or anything?" I questioned awkwardly. *Fran,* I thought, *you are such a jerk making stupid small talk like that. Why would you ask her about clubs of all things?*

Nancy was mercifully kind. My social ineptitude didn't seem to faze her in the least. I wondered what it must be like to be unselfconscious. In a little while, Nancy and her mother went back to Nan's room to finish putting away her things.

When it was time for Mom and Dad to leave, I walked them downstairs to the car and kissed them goodbye. "Enjoy yourself, honey," Mom said, squeezing me.

Dad gave me a hug and a kiss, then admonished, "Work hard, and think what I would say before you make any decisions. That way you'll do just fine."

I took a deep breath and exhaled slowly as I watched them drive away. Ploddingly, I made the four-flight trek back up to my room, and plunked myself down on the freshly made bed. I was anxious to explore Boston, go shopping, buy myself a new bedspread and some curtains, and hang some posters. Originally I had thought this would be something I would do with my new roommate, but since I didn't have one, I figured I could decorate however I wanted.

Unfortunately, I wasn't brave enough to inspect the city alone, so the first hurdle would be to force myself to be friendly to these girls who would be my suitemates. *Am I the only one with a past?* I wondered. I was sure I was, and held my secret closely. I tried desperately to fight the tears that threatened to overtake me. My fear of being completely alone was only complicated more by the belief that I truly was trapped in my solitude.

My reverie was interrupted by a young woman who bounced into the room. "Hi, I'm Chris Meyer," she welcomed me. "You're a freshman?"

"Yup, I'm Fran Gruss," I answered. "What class are you in?"

"I'm a junior from Maine," she offered. "You'll get used to it here soon enough. You might even get to like it," she laughed.

"I think I will like it," I said. "It's just so big, and there are so many kids here. I'm glad this is a small dorm."

"The small dorm helps," Chris stated, "but, the biggest problem here is all the Jews from New York."

I gasped. I had not counted on being greeted with anti-Semitism in my first fifteen minutes of college life! I pulled myself up from my relaxed stance and looked Chris Meyer in the eye. "Well, I'm Jewish," I stated confidently, "and that is one of the reasons I chose to come here."

Chris was as surprised as I had been. "Oh, oh," she stammered. "Your name, and you . . . well . . . don't look Jewish. I only meant I feel outnumbered here and . . . "

Her attempt at recovery was failing miserably. "I've got to go," she waved as she exited the room.

I thought to myself, *I guess I handled that pretty well. Maybe I will be okay. I'll just make myself talk to people, and they will just talk right back. I could never be as insensitive as that boor Chris was.*

Before long, I had not only met, but befriended the other girls in the suite. Shelby was a sophisticated New Yorker with a mane of strawberry blond hair. She had certainly been around, and when I heard that she had been smoking pot in the dorm, I was astounded. In 1965, marijuana had not found its way to suburban Norwalk, at least not to anyone I knew. I pretty much kept my distance from Shelby, remembering my father's reproof about avoiding the appearance of wrongdoing, and staying away from trouble.

Gabby was a theater major, and with her great beauty and fabulous figure, she looked much older than her eighteen years. Gabby was never without a date, and young men called for her constantly. The other two were art majors, and I watched with envy as they did their creative projects for class. We spent lots of time together, fooling around, going into the city to shop, and going to mixers.

I became closer to Nancy than to the others in our suite. There was a comfort and trust with her that went both ways, and I admired her social ease. The first week we were at school, as we sat in the soda shop at the pharmacy near the dorm, she whispered to me. "Look at that guy behind the counter. I'm going to get him to ask me out." Sure enough, within days, she had managed to fulfill her fantasy, and before very long they were constant companions.

I worked hard at my classes, harder than I'd ever imagined working in high school. I was a member of the honors program, and the work was extremely challenging. At home, if I'd had a problem with my schoolwork, Dad was always there to help. Here I was pretty much on my own, and at times I felt overwhelmed by the load. I was proud when I did reasonably well while still finding time to make a social life for myself.

The girls who didn't have steady boyfriends would spend weeknights at the library in an effort to meet other singles who were there for the same purpose. When I went to the library, I managed to get some work done, and still play the mixing game. From time to time, I would see Ronnie, my old friend from home, but by the end of first semester, he had transferred to another school. Once in a while I'd bump into Paul on campus, and managed to fix him up with one of my suitemates. They liked each other a lot, and that made me feel good.

Bob Lipton was a junior who lived in the apartment building next door. He was cute and playful, and I enjoyed flirting with him. He and his roommate, Bob Black, were always partying and having a good time. Neither of them was interested in having any kind of meaningful relationship, but they were very intent on socializing with the girls next door. It was easy to run over to their apartment, sit around casually and watch TV, eat a snack or listen to music. The familiarity and easy boy-girl banter was stimulating.

I was taken with Bob Lipton's breezy attitude, and I could tell he enjoyed my company. Occasionally, he would ask me to type his papers, in exchange for which he would take me out to dinner. The first time he kissed me, I was puzzled by my reaction. It was a combination of forbidden pleasure and overwhelming guilt. My body had not responded to a kiss in more than two years, and it frightened me. I continued to have this on again, off again relationship with Bob, in spite of the fact that I knew it would go nowhere. I never allowed him to get too close, terrified it would lead to a sexual encounter. I was determined to live as if I were still a virgin.

Bob never took me very seriously, and on more than one occasion I would look out my window on a weekend evening to the sight and sounds of him coming home with other girls. I couldn't allow Bob's lack of commitment to matter. If my dates or my boyfriends were not Jewish, there was no way I could tell my parents about them anyway. I had to pretend that those relationships did not exist.

By second semester, I had befriended some students who lived in a rooming house across the street from the dorm. One of them was a spirited sophomore named Jonathan. He was an international relations major from Wisconsin, with a mop of curly blond hair, and deep dimples in both cheeks. Jonathan made it clear he was interested in me. I started spending lots of time with him at the rooming house. Sometimes a large group of us would gather in the lounge and cook meals; at other times we would go to individual rooms to be alone to talk or study.

I was comfortable talking to Jonathan, but I still held back. As Jonathan became more romantic, I began to loosen up a little. There was still no way I would consider becoming physically intimate with him, and the frustration frequently left me in tears. Jonathan was obviously very confused by my behavior, but his laissez-faire attitude was reassuring. I was probably more confused than he was. I had a deep need for the kind of emotional intimacy I had shared with Ken, yet I could not allow myself to become physically intimate again. And wedged right in the center of that was my big secret.

In retrospect, I suspect Jonathan was probably more interested in a physical relationship than an emotional one, so he remained challenged by me. I felt thoroughly dishonest, yet remembered my father's admonition about protecting the family and remaining loyal to it by never divulging what had happened to me.

Early in the day on March 4, I received a phone call from my father. Dad never called me. As a matter of fact, it had been our habit that I would call home every Sunday morning, so this phone call on a Friday morning alerted me that something was very wrong. The minute he began talking I knew it wasn't good news.

"Fran," Dad said solemnly, "Grandma Ceil has had a heart attack, and she died."

"Oh, no," I cried, "it's not true." Grandma and Grandpa were spending their second winter in Florida. Grandma had experienced a mild heart attack several weeks before, but had been discharged from the hospital with every indication that she would be fine. Evidently, she was not.

"Daddy, she can't be gone. I'm supposed to go to Florida in a couple of weeks for Spring Break to be with them." My mind began racing. I couldn't think straight. *Get control of yourself, Fran,* I thought.

Dad was very clear about the plans that followed.

"Fran, I want you to take the train home. Uncle Larry will pick you up at the station. Mommy and I will be meeting Grandpa Irving at the airport. The funeral will be Sunday, so get your things together for a few days."

I did as I was told. In a daze, I packed my bags, took a cab to the railroad station, and made the four-hour rail journey home. The weather was dreary, and as I looked out the window my mind wandered to the special bond I had enjoyed with my cherished grandmother. Occasionally I would begin to cry, then check myself, realizing I was in a public place and it was important to exercise self-control.

As the reveries formed, I thought of the summer days I had spent with Grandma at camp, the weekends we had shared in Connecticut, and the months, day in and day out, when she and Grandpa had harbored me during my confinement. *My baby will be two years old this week, I realized. I wonder what he or she looks like, if everything is okay . . .* Then it hit me. Could the stress of maintaining my secret, of lying to Uncle Jay and abandoning him when he was in the hospital with his own heart attack . . . could that have caused her heart attack? If so, I was responsible for her death. It was my fault her life had ended prematurely at only sixty-five years old.

My tears fell unchecked now. I would never again find comfort in her warm bosom, or hear her soothing words as she patted my head and cradled me. I would never again hear her funny backwards sneezes or her silly laugh. *It was my fault. It was one more thing I had done to ensure the ruination of our family.*

The next week went by in a murky haze. I returned to school in shock. My friends were sympathetic, my professors less so. I had to get on with my life. Guilt added upon guilt, shame upon shame. I now had one more sin to add to my list. How much more perfect would I have to be to re-deem myself now?

I spent spring break in Florida with Grandpa Irving, sorting through Grandma's things, boxing them up to be sent home. Wistfully, we ate the food that Grandma had so carefully prepared and frozen away. Each bite reminded me this would be the last time I would taste things the way she made them. Grandpa and I cried and reminisced together. We never spoke of my contribution to her untimely death.

Mercifully, the end of the semester went quickly, and I returned home to Norwalk for the summer.

CHAPTER 12
Road Trip

I spent the summer of 1966 at home, taking some courses at a nearby university and hanging out with Amy. I met Edie in the city once or twice, drove down to New Jersey to see Nancy, and spent a weekend with another friend in Westchester.

Early in the summer, I began dating Harry, a "nice Jewish boy" of whom my parents approved. When he went away for a few weeks, he wrote me faithfully, and when he returned he seemed determined to see me more often. Harry was several years older than I and had just finished college. While he was sweet, I didn't experience anything resembling strong feelings for him, and I was definitely not interested in seeing him exclusively.

Midway through the summer, Amy and I decided to go to the Newport Folk Festival. I was excited about going away, seeing famous bands and singers up close, and just being with lots of other young people. Dad lent me his car, told me to drive carefully, and to keep in touch.

Once on the road, Amy looked at me. "I'm meeting Rick in Newport, Fran." It didn't surprise me she would make plans to do that. Her parents did not like her relationship with her non-Jewish boyfriend, yet Amy and Rick had been inseparable since the senior prom in high school. Their colleges were close to each other, so they were accustomed to spending lots of time together.

"Well, then," I said impulsively. "Let's stop in Boston first and see Jonathan at work. Maybe I can get him to come down, too." While Dad never would have approved, it suddenly didn't make any difference to me. I was twenty years old, and I wanted to have a harmless good time with my friends. Besides, the last thing I wanted was to be alone while Amy and Rick were together.

Jonathan was happy to see me. He thought it would be fun to go to the festival and spend some time together. I told him I'd call him as soon as I knew where we were staying, and he said he'd meet us there. I was elated. It was the first spontaneous thing I'd done in what seemed like forever, and it felt deliciously impetuous.

Because we didn't have room reservations anywhere, Amy and I drove until we were about an hour from Newport, stopping at a roadside place that advertised a vacancy. We figured we couldn't get much closer without paying a much higher price for the proximity to Newport.

Amy made arrangements to meet Rick at the festival, and Jonathan planned to come to meet us after work. Excitedly, we joined the throngs of fans—other young adults like ourselves at the festival—the beginning of the age of worship of music, youth, and the psychedelic life-style.

The evening was more eye opening than anything I had ever experienced. To actually see the bands up close, to hear the familiar strains live and sing along with the music was thrilling.

When the show ended, we went back to the car for the long ride back to the motel. The heavy traffic moved slowly and erratically. Somehow, Rick maneuvered his car behind mine, and we agreed that he and Amy would follow behind me. Eventually, traffic started to move, and I picked up a bit of speed. Then, without warning, the car in front of me decelerated abruptly. I slammed my foot on the brake, and in that instant, the car behind me, carrying Rick and Amy, smashed into mine.

I started to shake. Somehow, we both managed to pull over to the side of the road to inspect the damage. My rear bumper was smashed pretty badly, and the thought of having to deal with my father was frightening to me.

Amy and Rick tried to reassure me. "Don't worry," Amy said. "We'll work this out. None of us is hurt, your car is drivable, and Jonathan is expecting you."

Temporarily, I pushed aside my anxiety because Jonathan was waiting for me. When we arrived at the motel, Amy and Rick went immediately to their room.

Jonathan was sitting in his car, and grinned playfully when he saw me. But the stress of the evening finally overwhelmed me, and I began to cry. Jonathan embraced me and allowed me to vent my fear and distress. We entered the room, still holding fast to each other, and Jonathan kissed me tenderly. Relief flooded through me. As long as he held me, everything would be okay. His kisses became more demanding, and I felt my body tingle with desire. Finally, I couldn't take anymore, and I begged him to stop. "What's wrong?" he asked, totally confused.

"I can't," I said. "I can't go all the way."

"You always do this," he retorted. "You're so responsive, like you are really wanting me, and then you tell me to stop. I don't get it."

My tears resumed. How could I tell him the truth? How could I explain that I'd committed the ultimate sin with someone else, and as much as I cared for him, I couldn't bring myself to do it again? And what if he knew I'd had a baby? No way. Not now. I couldn't say the words.

"I just can't. Please understand. I need you to just hold me."

So Jonathan held me. I felt comforted and managed to preserve my status as a nice girl—whatever that meant.

The next morning, the four of us ate breakfast together. "What am I going to tell my father about the car?" I asked.

Amy and Rick looked conspiratorially at each other. "Well, you can't tell your dad that Rick did it," Amy answered. "If my parents knew I met him up here, they'd kill me."

How could I lie to my father about this? It was one thing to take a detour to Boston, to meet Jonathan; I could simply leave that part out. But to lie to him directly about how the accident happened? I wasn't sure I could pull that off.

"Tell him it was a hit and run," Rick suggested.

"How could I say that? I'd have to describe the car. Amy and I would have to match stories. It's too risky, I can't," I demurred.

"What about saying you got hit in the parking lot?" Jonathan proposed. "You could say you got back to the car after the concert, and found it that way."

"I suppose, but I'm really uncomfortable about this."

"It looks like you don't have much choice," Amy said coolly.

We finished our breakfast, but to me, the fun had been erased from the weekend. We said lingering goodbyes to Rick and Jonathan, and left for home. In the car, Amy and I didn't do much talking. I was so confused. I didn't want to lie to my father. I had promised I would redeem myself in his eyes. What if I got caught in a lie?

Amy was adamant. "If you tell your father that Rick was the one who hit you, my parents will find out. I can't let that happen. Fran, if you tell him it was Rick, I'll have to tell your father you spent the night with Jonathan."

A chill went through me. Dad would be furious. Even though Jonathan and I didn't have sex, he would never believe me, never trust me again. I couldn't take that chance.

"Okay, Amy. You win. I'll use the story that I was hit in the parking lot." I was so angry I could no longer speak. I was furious with her for coercing me that way, and I was furious with myself for putting myself in the position of having to tell lie upon lie to keep the myth of my redemption going.

Fortunately, my father did not question my story about the car being hit in the parking lot. His insurance covered the damage, and the event slid by. Eventually, I stopped feeling so anxious about being found out, and managed to get on with my summer and resume my long-held friendship with Amy.

One day before I went back to school, I was reading the local newspaper, as I usually did in the afternoon, and saw an article on the society page that made me gasp. It was a wedding announcement. Ken was married. I couldn't believe it. How had this happened? He was supposed to wait for me. He promised he would love me forever and no one else would ever have his love. I was devastated. What else could I do now but move on as he had?

CHAPTER 13

Explorations of the Heart

*I*t was September, and I returned to college to live in a brand new high-rise dormitory. I roomed with a girl who had lived downstairs from me in the old dorm. She was a business major, and had lots of friends. We got along pretty well, and though I would have preferred to live with Nancy, she had made other arrangements with a dance major named Ruth from New York. Ruth purportedly "needed" her more than I did. In truth, Nancy didn't know how much I truly did need her.

As the year progressed, I continued to date both Jonathan and Bob on and off, occasionally seeing other young men as well. I longed to meet someone with whom I could have a deeper relationship, but it didn't happen. My loneliness at times overwhelmed me. I thought about Ken often, wondering about his new life, imagining that things would be different . . . maybe someday . . . I would graduate from college, be an adult; we could find our way back to each other . . . I prayed something might happen to bring us together again . . . but how could that be? He was married. It was completely impossible.

Later in the school year, I received a note from my friend Paul, who had graduated from BU and was now attending law school in Washington, DC. At his invitation, I went there to visit him. I was pleased that he wanted to continue our friendship, and wondered if perhaps he was interested in me. He certainly was nice looking and smart; my parents definitely approved of him.

We spent a wonderful weekend. He showed me all the famous landmarks and I was in awe of the beauty of the city. Paul clearly loved law school, and was dedicated to furthering the cause of civil rights. He told me his plans for the following summer were to go down south to help the freedom riders integrate public facilities. I was impressed with his dedication and independence. I wondered if I would ever be brave enough to take a risk like that. The time spent with Paul had been exhilarating, but it was obvious that his interest in me was purely platonic. It was good to have a friend like Paul, and that was okay with me.

Before I knew it, the school year was over. I made arrangements to stay in Boston for the summer and live in an apartment with a girl named Eileen. I would work in the business department of the university (where my secretarial training would serve me well) and take a couple of classes. I was twenty-one years old, working, and living in my own apartment. Even if it was just for the summer, I felt very mature and liberated.

Eileen and I got along well. She was easy-going and garrulous, and attracted people with her charming Canadian accent, tiny stature, and sultry eyes. Eileen and I enjoyed going out together on nights she didn't already have a date. We'd go to clubs, and the minute we sat down, she would be surrounded by a host of attractive young men. I wished I knew her secret.

Our apartment was wonderful. We lived in a first floor unit that faced Commonwealth Avenue. It had a huge bow window that overlooked the street. There was a tiny kitchenette, and a single bedroom. We spent hours in that living room with the stereo playing and the windows open so the summer breeze could cool us.

I enjoyed my job in the business school. The professor whom I was assisting was pleased with my work, and I was never bored.

I particularly enjoyed my summer school classes. I was taking Spanish 101, and it was there I met Andy Klein. He was a charming, self-assured student in the six-year medical school program. Our teacher was a lovely young Argentinian woman who made learning easy and enjoyable. I would tease Andy about having a crush on her, and he laughed—never denying he was interested in her.

Andy and I spent leisurely lunches together, studied together, and became good friends. I was challenged by his intelligence and wit, and enjoyed bantering and flirting with him.

One day in class, the teacher asked us questions in Spanish about ourselves. "*Quantos anos tienes tu, Andy?*" she queried.

"Yo tengo diez y ocho anos," he responded.

My heart dropped. He was only eighteen years old? How could that be? He was in the medical program. I couldn't possibly be three years older than he. It seemed like so much of a difference. Yet he was mature and sophisticated, and extremely attractive.

Later he explained, "I graduated high school right after I turned seventeen. I had skipped a year, and then I was admitted to the six-year med program. I'll be a doctor at twenty-three."

I was incredulous. I knew Andy was bright, but this really threw me. I enjoyed his company, but . . .

"Andy, I'm twenty-one," I said cautiously.

"Lots of my friends are older," he replied. "It's no big deal."

It sure felt like a big deal to me. I enjoyed his company, and had met several of his friends, and enjoyed them too. But the taboo about older girls and younger guys was so strong, and the thought of dating him made me uncomfortable. I found myself pulling back and fighting the feelings that had begun to grow in me.

At the end of August I received horrible news. Paul had been murdered in Mississippi. He had been there as he planned, working for the civil rights effort. One night, on his way home, his car was forced off the road, and he was killed in the crash. His killers were never apprehended.

The loss of my friend was incomprehensible. How could such talent, such passion and drive just be ended like that? For a life to be cut short just as it was beginning to make a difference didn't make any sense to me. The sadness I felt resonated with the other losses I had experienced. Each one was so different, yet they weighed heavily on me.

Summer school ended, and it was autumn. My roommate and I decided not to room together again, and I took a single room in the high-rise. This way I could be near my friends, yet still have quiet and privacy when I wanted it.

I was a junior now. I decided to change my major from elementary to secondary education. I believed I could make a difference to high school students. My experience as an adolescent was still fresh in my mind and I knew I could never forget what it was like to be a teenager. I trusted that this knowledge would enable me to reach out and make a difference in my students' lives, touching them so they would feel less alone and know someone understood and cared about them.

Jonathan transferred to the University of Hawaii that semester, and his letters dwindled to post cards, then nothing. As the memory of Jonathan faded, my friendship with Andy grew, even though I continued to hold back.

One beautiful Sunday afternoon in October, we took a walk along the Charles River. The sun was glorious, the leaves golden-red, the sailboats and crew teams abundant on the river. As we talked, Andy took my hand. A shiver ran through me, and my stomach did a tumble.

"You know, Fran, we've been friends for some time now," he said. "I hope you know I feel something more than friendship for you."

"I know," I answered, "I've been feeling that too."

We stopped walking and turned to one another. Andy purposefully leaned toward me and kissed me. I felt my resolve melt at that moment, and knew that our relationship would never be the same again.

We walked back to his dormitory where Sunday visiting hours were in effect. That meant I was allowed in his room—so long as the door was open and four feet remained on the floor. His suitemates greeted me warmly, and I felt reassured that his bringing me here affirmed his feelings for me. We kissed and snuggled for the rest of the afternoon, and Andy assured me I was "his girl."

Andy was one of the more popular members of his fraternity. Many of the members were, like Andy, pre-med students, and they were an active group who participated in many activities in the Boston area. In addition to having clean good looks, Andy sang and played the guitar. His smooth voice and confident bearing endeared him to his peers and turned more than a few female heads.

I quickly settled into the routine of being a "little sister" to the fraternity members. They acknowledged me as Andy's girlfriend, and I developed my own friendships with several of the young men.

I had finally reached a point where I was comfortable with my male peers without being nervous. I knew how they felt about me because they told me—and I knew I was good for Andy. He told me he enjoyed having intellectual conversations with me, as well as having a pretty girlfriend.

Andy had dated another girl before me, and I was aware that he some-times still saw her. But I refused to let that bother me. "You are Andy's girlfriend," his friend Louis exhorted. "Don't worry about Michelle; she's the past and you're right now."

Andy and I continued happily as a couple, and made plans to see each other during winter break. On New Year's Eve he drove to Connecticut and picked me up, and we traveled back to Long Island for dinner and a party. I met his parents and they treated me warmly. It was obvious that Andy had told them how much he cared about me.

Soon we were back at school again, and settled into our routines. During the week we would meet for a quick cup of coffee or a study date. We'd find a quiet corner of the library stacks and do our work, tak-ing breaks every so often to get a snack or kiss until it was time to study again. On Saturday afternoons we would go into Boston to explore a mu-seum or shop, or I would watch him rehearse with his singing ensemble, and on Saturday nights we would go to a movie or a fraternity party.

We spent leisurely Sunday afternoons together in his room, avoiding the resident assistant who was charged with enforcing the rules. It felt so good to watch television, listen to music and just relax while holding each other.

Sometimes our kissing would go further than I could handle, and I would panic. *I can't let this go on,* I would tell myself. But being held by him, feeling close to him, was what I ached to experience again. Andy was tender and patient. He never challenged my reticence to go further, and as time went by I trusted him more and more.

Finally, one Sunday afternoon early in the spring, my resolve broke, and Andy and I finally made love. It had been five years since I had trust-ed anyone enough to allow that much intimacy. It was so simple. I trust-ed him, and trusted our relationship. I allowed myself to finally feel the pleasure of intimacy, but when it was over, I cried.

Andy attributed my tears to the deepening of our relationship, and soothed me. "It's okay Fran. I . . . I love you," he whispered.

"And I love you," I returned. "I hope you're not disappointed in me."

"How could I be?" he replied. "You're wonderful."

Why, at nearly twenty-two years old, did I not feel like an adult wom-an? Why, even though he was younger, did I look to Andy for sanction and approval of my worth and respect? I had yet to prove those things to myself. My guilt notwithstanding, we remained a couple, closer than ever.

Shortly after that, on Andy's nineteenth birthday, a pall fell over the campus when we learned of the murder of Dr. Martin Luther King. Because we were so committed to civil rights, we felt the blow acutely and wondered how this setback would affect us all. We headed into final exams and prepared for the summer ahead.

Andy and I both decided to remain in Boston for the summer to take classes. I moved into Nancy's apartment in Brookline, and a few of our friends lived right across the hall. By this time, Nancy was spending most of her time at her fiancé's apartment, and they were planning to be married in June. I could have the apartment with her roommate, Ruth, until the end of the summer. Andy took an apartment with two of his fraternity brothers, a couple of blocks away.

In time, the comfortable stability of my relationship with Andy began to erode. He rarely told me he loved me, and I couldn't understand his need to spend more time away from me. The only time I felt truly close to him was when we made love. I still found myself in tears every time, and we talked about my emotions at great length. I had an overwhelming need to feel secure. I realized that the biggest problem with our age difference was that I wanted to settle down for life, and he still had lots to do before he could make that commitment.

Our mutual friend Louis shed some light on the situation. "Andy's mother is very unhappy with your relationship," he offered. "He still has years of medical school ahead of him, and she bugs him all the time about going out with other girls."

"How can I contend with that?" I lamented.

"Andy loves you," Louis said, supportively. "I know it."

One night in early June, I spent the night in Andy's arms. I wanted to hold him close. My secret was beginning to weigh more and more heavily on me. I considered sharing it with Andy. If he could forgive my sin, I knew it would bring us closer together. Again our lovemaking brought me to tears, and he gently soothed me. "Frani, what is it? Why are you crying?"

"I have to tell you something . . . it's important, and I don't know how you'll feel about it."

"I care about you . . . it's all right, honey." I took a deep breath and poured out my story.

"I had a baby four years ago, and had to give it up for adoption." Silence answered me. There were no words Andy could offer that would stop the pounding in my chest. My body went cold, and I began to tremble. *Was this the end?* Finally, the warmth of his arms returned and he held me closely.

"Oh, Frani," he murmured, "don't worry."

"Are you sure?" I pleaded. "You don't hate me? We're still okay?"

"Don't worry. We're fine," he answered.

But I had the overwhelming sense that we wouldn't be fine. I was certain I had made a big mistake by telling him.

My fears seemed to be coming true as I saw less and less of Andy. Nancy was getting ready to go home to be married, and I was in the depths of depression. One evening, I sat in the window of my second floor apartment and stared out into the darkness. Where was Andy? Why couldn't he make a commitment to me?

I needed so desperately to feel loved and accepted. I had told Andy my dreaded secret, and now he was gone. I felt so betrayed. *Wasn't I good enough? Why hadn't Kenny fought for our love? Why hadn't he waited? Was I so worthless? I can't go on. I want to die,* I told myself.

The tears began to fall unremittingly. Nancy walked into the room and saw how distraught I was. "What's wrong, Fran?"

I couldn't stop crying. "I want to die," I wept. "I can't go on anymore."

"Fran, tell me," she pleaded. "What's happened?"

My mind was a blur. How could I explain to her about the painful emotions boiling over in my mind, in my heart? If I told her she'd have no respect for me . . . she'd leave me the way Andy did, and I'd be alone again.

"Fran, no matter what it is, it will be all right. I'm your friend, and I want to help you." She held me, and I felt comforted by her words. But the panic, the fear would not leave me.

"Andy is gone, and it's because of something I told him. It's terrible," I sobbed, "and if I tell you, you'll hate me, too."

"That's impossible," she maintained. "I won't hate you. We're friends, real friends, and friends are there for each other. You've always been there for me, haven't you? Even when I wasn't so pleasant to you . . . you didn't give up on me, did you? Our friendship is solid, you have to know that."

Finally, she wore me down. Sobbing, the words came tumbling out. "I told him . . . I told him . . . I can't, I can't."

"Yes you can, Fran, I'm here for you," she consoled.

I began again. "Remember how I told you I went away in high school? Remember I said my parents made me break up with Kenny and I threatened to run away? So they pulled me out of school and sent me away with my grandparents. It was a lie . . . I went away to have his baby . . . he never knew . . . I had to . . . to give it up. I had a baby and I had to give it up. I told Andy, and now he's left me. I just want to die." I was choking with the sobs that racked my body.

"Fran, I'm so sorry," she comforted. "What a dreadful thing to happen to you."

As she held me in her arms I felt the sincerity of her compassion. "I'm sure that Andy just isn't mature enough to handle a relationship with you. You're a woman, and he's still a kid. Your secret is safe with me, I promise you. And I'll always be here for you. I will always be your friend, and you can always talk to me."

Relief flooded over me. Nancy truly was my friend. She would be there for me, and I could go on. I could make a life for myself. But the gnawing wouldn't go away . . . Nancy had something on me. I hoped she wouldn't ever use it. I was terrified that she too would betray my trust.

I went alone to Nancy's wedding. The parallels between my former relationship with Ken and this marriage were not lost on me. Nancy was Jewish, her husband Catholic. Somehow they had worked it out. Her parents had not disowned her. They were planning a life together. He was going into the army, and they would be living in Frankfurt for a year. If my dearest friend who was a full year younger than I was an adult—old enough to get married to the man she loved and go to live in Europe on her own—what was wrong with me that I didn't feel I could do anything on my own? I wondered why I still needed the unfettered approval of my parents. Would I ever grow up?

In July, my childhood friend Edie got married in New York. I traveled home again, and this time I brought a date with me. One of Andy's roommates was happy to accompany me. He and his girlfriend hadn't been getting along too well, and he was only too happy to get out of town for a while. I was happy with the no-pressure, just-friends kind of date.

I hadn't met Edie's fiancé before the wedding, and I was pleased to see how nice he was. He was friendly and good-looking, and they seemed so content. I wished them well, and told her I would see her again at the end of the summer. They were setting up housekeeping in the Bronx, and Edie was beginning her teaching career there.

I was still acutely aware of my lies to my friends about the reasons for my disappearance, but they never mentioned it. Nancy was in Germany, so I didn't have to worry about her betraying my confidence—at least not for now. But it was always on my mind.

I returned to Boston determined I would begin to make my life more satisfying. I met several different young men who flirted with me and whose company I enjoyed. Jerry lived in the building next door, and we met in the laundry room. He regaled me with stories of his unsatisfying relationship with his girlfriend, and how he wished she were more like me.

Once I bumped into Bob on campus, and went for a ride with him. We got a bite to eat, then went back to his place. I let him kiss me, and allowed myself to feel the excitement of being close to someone again, but ended up feeling guilty and cheap. I didn't want to be an easy pickup—I wanted someone to love me. Besides, I still had feelings for Andy.

Ben was a law student who lived in the apartment downstairs, and continually pressured me to go out with him. Rather than spend nights alone, I sometimes went to dinner or a movie with him, or just sat and talked. Ben was kind to me. He never forced himself on me, and was patient with my radical mood swings.

But whenever Andy called, I would go running. It was as if he couldn't give me up, but couldn't make a commitment either. I was totally committed to him, and wanted him to know that I loved him. One night I broke a date with Ben and instead went to Andy's, spending the night there. As I came in the next morning, Ben met me on the stairs. He was frantic.

"You were with him again?" I didn't answer, aware of the pain in his eyes. "How can you be with him when he treats you like that, Fran? Don't you know I would never do that to you . . . that I love you?"

I swallowed and took a deep breath. "Oh, Ben . . . I'm so sorry. I didn't mean to hurt you. You've been such a good friend to me. But . . . I'm not, I can't. You should be with someone who can love you the way you deserve . . . who'll be devoted to you. I'm moving to Cambridge in a few weeks—school will be starting again and you won't have to see me. I truly am sorry. It's just that I love Andy, whatever the terms."

And I knew then, because I had to admit it to myself, that because I loved him, I would take Andy however I could, even if it wasn't the way I wanted it to be. Andy's friends continued to treat me warmly. It was as if they accepted me even when he couldn't.

I found an apartment in a brand new building in Cambridge where Ruth, Nancy's former roommate, and I would live for our senior year. Ruth was spending almost all her time at her boyfriend's apartment, so we found a third roommate, a likable girl who worked at a department store. The three of us got along well.

In addition, three of Andy's friends took an apartment downstairs from me. I never felt alone, and there was always a friendly face and an ear to listen when I needed one.

CHAPTER 14

Vanquishing My Past

*S*hortly before classes began for my senior year, I went home for the weekend to visit, and Dad surprised me with a car of my own.

"You'll need the car for student teaching," he said "and it will make it easier to come back and forth. Besides, honey," he said proudly, "you've earned it."

If only he knew, I thought. He'd be so disappointed in me if he knew about the nature of my relationship with Andy, and my having betrayed the family secret by telling not only Andy, but Nancy as well. I kept my thoughts to myself. Neither of my parents, or anyone for that matter, ever mentioned the past. I certainly wasn't going to jeopardize my present or my future by disclosing what the "real" Fran was doing.

Mom, Dad, and I went to the movies that weekend, and as we were leaving, we saw Dad's cousins, Gene and Frances. It had been some time since I'd seen them, and they gushed over how great I looked.

"You're twenty-two now?" Frances asked.

"Yes, I'm starting my senior year," I replied.

"Well," Gene offered, "We hope you'll be able to come to our son's Bar Mitzvah in November. There's someone we want you to meet."

Oh no, I thought, *they want to fix me up. What about Andy?* I mused in my head, but didn't say anything.

"David is my cousin on my father's side, and just a bit older than you. I think you would like each other." He smiled mischievously.

"Gene," his wife interrupted, "don't embarrass her. Honey, we'd love to have you there. David is pretty cute, though."

"I'm sure I'll be able to come," I answered. "I always enjoy family celebrations." *Maybe David would be an interesting diversion, I thought.*

I began my last year of college with enthusiasm. I took courses I loved and was well on my way to realizing my dream as a social studies teacher. Edie inspired me with stories about her classes, and I couldn't wait to begin teaching. I still saw Andy occasionally, but even more rarely than before. Somehow, though, his friends lifted my spirits, and the excitement of my classes acted as a distraction from the intense emotions I had felt during the summer.

On Thanksgiving weekend I went home for the annual family festivities, and that Saturday we all attended the Bar Mitzvah of Gene and Frances' son. I dressed in a short, slightly flared yet fitted, deep brown dress with long sleeves and dozens of tiny covered buttons parading up the back onto the turtleneck. My hair was smoothed into a flip, and my make-up trendy Twiggy style. As I entered the reception, I looked around the room, knowing I looked good.

A cheerful, friendly man I didn't know ran to greet my father. "Marty, how are you? It's been so many years."

Dad answered him warmly. "Lou, how are you?"

"Wonderful," he responded.

"I understand you have a daughter." He regarded me eagerly. "Come, I have a son."

I was embarrassed by Lou's attention, but it was obvious he had been told by Gene and Frances I would be there. I followed his gaze and saw David standing at the bar. He had one foot up on the foot rail and was leaning into avid conversation with Jenny, his ten-year-old cousin. He wore a double-breasted brown suit and looked very handsome with a wave of soft brown hair across his brow, his face punctuated by aviator glasses.

Awkwardly, Lou introduced us, and then our families left us to chat. Blessedly, Jenny remained with us and acted as a buffer and some welcome release from our discomfort. When it came time to sit down to dinner, David and I were both shocked to discover that we had been seated at the children's table.

The only respite from our awkwardness and the follies of the thirteen-year-olds around us was the conversation engendered by David's nineteen-year-old sister Shari, who was also seated with us. Before the afternoon was over, however, David and I relaxed and enjoyed some easy conversation. When he asked me for my phone number, I wasn't surprised, and was happy to give it to him.

I went back to school on Sunday, knowing I would be hearing from him and wondering what impact this new man in my life would have on my relationship with Andy.

David managed to call me a couple of times a week, and made it clear that he wanted a real date when I came home for Christmas break.

As final exams started, I began feeling ill. I started to run a fever, was dizzy and weak, and couldn't even get out of bed. I missed several of my tests, as did many other students, due to the outbreak of the Hong Kong flu. How was I going to get home?

Eventually, I had the idea to call Amy in Providence and enlist her help. She took the train to Boston, came to my apartment, and drove us both home to Norwalk in my car. Finally I was back home in my own bed, and my mother could tend to me and bring me chicken soup and nurse me back to health.

Despite my illness, David insisted on visiting. He called me and said he would be coming on Saturday, and while we didn't have to go out, he just wanted to see me. I primped as best as I could in my weakened condition, and hoped I didn't turn him off completely.

When he entered my room, he presented me with a small package. "Here's a little get well gift for you," he stated. I was so surprised by his thoughtfulness, and I opened it carefully. Inside was a beautiful silk scarf. It was white with a pattern of pink, green and turquoise swirls. Not only was he thoughtful, but he had good taste!

I thanked him profusely, and we talked some more until it was time for him to leave. He promised that we would have our real date as soon as I was well.

The following weekend David decided we might have fun going skeet shooting at a range about forty-five minutes north of my home. He picked me up mid-morning, and we got on the highway and headed to the shooting grounds. Unfortunately, when we arrived there we learned they were closed for the holiday season. David and I looked at each other, trying to decide what to do next.

"Well," I said, "we could always go to the mall."

"Great idea, Fran. Let's go. We can walk around, shop a little, and get something to eat."

We spent several hours window shopping, and returned to his car ready to go back to my home for dinner. As he opened the car door for me, he looked me in the eye, and bent ever so slightly to kiss me. It was a sweet kiss, full of promise, and I cautiously returned it. Without further discussion, we both smiled, and headed back.

After dinner, as we were saying our goodbyes, David asked me a question. "Do you have plans for New Year's? My friend Will is having a party in the city, and I'd really like you to come with me."

I hadn't even considered what would be happening for New Year's Eve—I suppose I was waiting for Andy to call and make arrangements. I hedged a little and said, "I had tentative plans, but they aren't firm. Let me get back to you in a day or two." I knew it wasn't very nice of me, but my emotions were in such turmoil I had to sit with my thoughts and feelings and think.

David smiled sweetly, and said, "Sure, just let me know. I'll be happy to come pick you up."

I was no closer to making a decision when I decided to just call Andy and see what his intentions were. I nervously dialed his number, and when he answered, my heart raced. "Andy, I met someone who asked me out for New Year's Eve. What should I tell him?"

Andy paused for a moment and gave me the answer I wasn't sure I wanted to hear.

"I think you should go with him." My dreams of repairing my relationship with Andy ended right there, and I decided that I would just see where things would go with David.

On New Year's Eve I spent a fun evening meeting David's friends, and by the time David took me home, we were totally comfortable with each other. I knew that we would be having many more special dates.

After I returned to school, David and I spoke nearly every day. He told me he wanted to come to Cambridge and visit me. Two weeks later, he flew into Boston, and I excitedly picked him up at the airport. As I greeted him at the gate, he beamed at me, and I was truly happy to see him. We kissed enthusiastically, and we drove directly to my apartment.

I was so proud of my place. I had decorated it myself, and the exposed brick walls, the sleek, yet spare modern furniture and the blue and yellow color scheme directly reflected my personality. David was impressed, and he put down his bags, and took me in his arms.

We kissed more urgently this time, and before I knew it we were in my bedroom. All the yearning, all the passion, all the insecurity that had built inside me had me clinging to this man as if my life depended on it. We made love, and I cried.

"Are you okay?" he worriedly asked.

"Yes, I'm okay. I'm just very emotional," I reassured him.

My brain was going a million miles an hour. Of course I was emotional. I loved Ken and he and our baby were gone. I loved Andy and he left me. Was I an awful person because I had made love with David? Would David leave me too?

The weekend turned out to be wonderful. I showed him all my favorite places in Boston. I cooked for him and enjoyed "playing house." We spent more than a few hours making love and holding each other in my little bed, and when it was time for him to return to New York, he assured me he would come back in a couple of weeks for Valentine's Day.

February 14 was a Friday. I picked David up at the airport early that evening, and we went straight back to my apartment. Immediately he pulled out a beautifully wrapped package and a card, beaming. I carefully opened the package to reveal a beautiful gold heart pin with a pearl nestled in it.

"It's beautiful, David, thank you so much."

"Fran, I want you to know that I love you."

"Oh, David, I love you too." And I truly did.

Just then the doorbell rang. Standing there with a huge bouquet of flowers and a gigantic oversized card, was Andy. My heart stopped. Andy stepped into the apartment, and I awkwardly introduced them. As they sized each other up, I wondered what all this meant.

David claimed his territory. "Nice to meet you, Andy. I'm here for the weekend visiting Fran."

The nineteen-year-old Andy sized up the twenty-four-year-old David, and it was obvious who was making the commitment. Andy eased toward the door, "Well, have a great weekend, you two."

"That was awkward," I gulped. "Not to worry, David. You are the man I love, and flowers and a big fancy card aren't going to change that."

We spent the rest of the weekend enjoying ourselves, and didn't discuss Andy again.

David and I made plans to go skiing in Vermont the following weekend. He was a member of a timeshare, and had monthly access to a ski house. The fact that I had never been skiing before did not deter either of us. The plan was for him to drive from New York to Cambridge, pick me up, and then drive us to Vermont. That next week I bought warm clothes, rented ski equipment, and planned for our first weekend away together.

The ski house was beautiful. It was a typical chalet structure with rustic wood walls and ceiling beams. There were several other young adults there who were members of the weekend share, and they greeted David and me cordially. My trips to northern New England had always been confined to summer vacations, so the winter magic of Stratton Mountain was intoxicating. Everything was blanketed in pristine snow, the roadsides crisply plowed into even mazes. We went for dinner the first night at a romantic restaurant that was famous for its juicy, plump butter drenched steaks.

After dinner we went back to the house and fell wearily into bed, excited about the next day, when I would experience my first time on skis.

The next morning dawned sparkling clear and cold. We dressed for the weather and drove to the resort. David arranged for me to take lessons while he skied the more challenging slopes. Knowing how much he loved it, I really tried to love it too, but the constant falling, my fear of hurting myself, and my distaste for being cold put a real damper on my enjoyment. We met back at the resort lodge for hot chocolate and planned to have dinner with the group back at the mountain house.

Dinner turned into a party, and all the other young adults were having a great time joking and dancing and drinking. Maybe because I was tired, cold and grumpy, I wasn't such fun to be with. I walked away from the group, and David followed me.

"What's wrong?" he asked.

"I don't know," I responded. "I guess I'm feeling very alone right now."

"But Fran, you're with me. You're not alone, and I love you."

"Really?" I said. "If you loved me so much you'd want to marry me."

Without a moment's hesitation, he said, "OK, let's get married."

"Are you serious? You really want to marry me?" I asked.

"Yes, I really want to marry you. So consider yourself engaged."

My mood lifted, and when he drove me back to Boston, all I could think about was that I had finally found someone who loved me and wanted to commit himself to me. Marrying David would somehow legitimize me, and vanquish my past.

I spent spring break at home in Norwalk, applying for teaching jobs for the fall. My birthday was coming up, and for a special treat, David had bought tickets to see the show *Hair* on Broadway.

In those days, it was a big deal to go to a Broadway show, and I got all dressed up in a beautiful white silk short dress with a blue velvet ribbon belt. When David came to pick me up he looked so handsome I was smitten all over again. We stood in the hallway outside my room, and he reached in his pocket and pulled out a beautiful diamond ring. As he slipped it on my finger, he said, "This makes it official. We're really engaged to be married."

"Oh, David, I'm so happy. It's beautiful; you are wonderful, and I can't wait to marry you." We went into the living room and proudly showed off my ring to my parents. My mother was beaming, yet my father was a little more reserved.

"Congratulations, you two. I hope you'll be very happy together," Dad said.

The next day, I asked my father why he had been so quiet. "I'm concerned, Fran. You and David come from different worlds. He doesn't have an education, his parents don't seem to have the same values we do, and I worry those things may get in the way of your marriage."

"What do you mean?" I asked. "What kind of values? They're Jewish like we are."

Dad explained, "His parents are older, they're more old-world and they don't have a lot of money. They're in a very different place than we are."

"It won't matter, Daddy. I love David and he loves me. We get along fine, and want the same things. That's what matters."

I knew what I wanted. I wanted a husband, a home, and children. Oh how I desperately wanted children. I asked David when we should get married. "How about August?" I suggested.

"That's way too soon, Fran. We haven't been together even a year yet."

"Well, how about during my Christmas break in December?"

"That sounds good, honey. Let's do it then."

I went back to Boston for the last month of college, ready to take on my adult life. One late afternoon, right before exams, there was a knock at the door. I opened it to see Andy standing there. Oh, no, I thought.

"Can I come in?" Andy asked.

"Sure, Andy, what is it?"

"I wanted to see you before graduation. I heard you got engaged."

"Yes, I did."

"I know that's what you always wanted, Fran—to get married and have a family. I'm sorry I wasn't in a place to give you those things, but I want you to know I hope you'll be very happy."

"Thank you for that Andy," I said. "It means a lot to hear you say that."

"Can I kiss you good bye?" he asked.

I pondered his request. What could it hurt? It would certainly give me some much needed closure.

"Yes," I said, "you can kiss me good bye." We put our arms around each other for a sweet and caring farewell to our relationship and all we had meant to one another. We were both finally ready to move on.

CHAPTER 15

A New Career and a New Life

*B*y the end of the first week in May 1969, I was a college graduate and had moved back home. I found a long-term substitute teaching job in Greenwich for the last month of school, and was excited to receive a call offering me a job at my old middle school in Norwalk for the fall. The principal at Western Middle School loved hiring his former students, and there were a number of alumni there who were working as teachers. I accepted the position, and eagerly spent the summer planning for my new assignment and shopping for my wedding.

The wedding was planned for December 21. Mom hired a caterer, an orchestra, and a florist, and decided the wedding would be in the synagogue affiliated with the school where she worked. All I had to do was make up my part of the invitation list, and choose the bridesmaids and the color scheme. This was to be Mom's big show, and the only other important decision I made was that there was to be no grapefruit in the fruit salad, because I disliked it. It was Mom who had the final say on my gown and the bridesmaid dresses, which had ice blue bodices and purple velvet skirts.

My first year of teaching began with a teachers' strike. All the new staff gathered in confusion, not knowing whether or not we would lose our jobs if we participated in the strike. After several days of negotiations, the union settled, and we were able to go back to work. Fortunately, there were to be no repercussions for the new people.

At the same time I started my new job, I eagerly entered my graduate school program, hoping I could get my master's degree as soon as possible.

At my first staff meeting, I looked around the cafeteria. Some of my old teachers were still there, and I was happy that I would be able to learn from and work with them side by side. Suddenly, I heard a familiar voice talking across the room. He was there—looking as handsome and vital as ever. It was Ken! He had become a math teacher as he had planned, and he was here, teaching in the same school

Mom and Dad, 1969.

as I was. The familiar knot grew in my stomach, but there was no escape this time. I couldn't leave the room. I couldn't run away.

The principal began introducing the new staff—"Fran Gruss, Social Studies." I stood up nervously and smiled while the assembled gathering applauded. I didn't dare make eye contact with Ken, but I could feel his eyes on me.

The next day, the students arrived, and we were thrust into the chaos of the beginning days of school. There were lots of new young teachers like me, and I quickly made friends with some of them. I saw Ken in passing at least once a day, but we rarely said more than a cordial "hi."

I was disappointed to be a "traveling teacher," meaning I didn't have my own classroom. I would use other teachers' rooms during their free periods, and use the Social Studies office as my home base. In October, due to some room changes, I found that once every day Ken and I occupied classrooms across the hall from each other. Because we had to be outside our classrooms during passing, we started to casually chat—first about nothing in particular, then changing to mild flirtation. I still got butterflies in my stomach every time I saw him, but couldn't get the nerve up to say anything to him of any importance.

One day, the pressure inside me built to such an extent I finally said something. "Ken, we have to talk. There's so much I have to tell you."

Getting ready for the wedding, December 1969.

"I know," he said, comfortingly. "We will." But the time never came.

December 21, 1969—the day of my wedding to David—was beautiful. The sun shone brightly on the unseasonably warm first day of winter. Sidra, David's sister Shari, and my friend Nancy were my bridesmaids. As I walked into the chapel on the arms of my parents, the sun's rays filtered through the stained glass windows and splayed a rainbow over the room's expanse. As I walked down the aisle I couldn't help but think I was making a big mistake. I had never told David about my secret—not so much because I didn't trust him, but because my shame was so deep I thought he couldn't possibly want me if he knew. I put it out of my mind. It was too late to change things now.

We had a spectacular, romantic honeymoon in Jamaica, and I returned to school in January with a new name. I was now Mrs. Levin.

Every year, in the spring, the days between the anniversary of my grandmother's death and my baby's birthday blurred together. In the solitude of the shower in the mornings, I would let the hot water rain down on me and I would cry until there were no more tears. This went on for weeks. I was grieving the loss of my baby alone, and no one could know.

One night in March of 1970, I experienced a bout of debilitating symptoms. I was in bed late at night when it started. My body was racked with chills, overwhelming nausea, stomach cramps, and heart palpitations that were unrelenting. I felt my way to the bathroom and collapsed in a heap on the floor next to the toilet. I felt like I was going to die. *It must be food poisoning,* I thought. Finally after about a half hour, the symptoms began to abate and I crawled back to bed. This was my first episode of these symptoms, but it was not to be my last.

In April, David and I moved into our own apartment. For the first few months of our marriage, we had saved some money by staying in the home of my Grandpa Abe and Grandma Esther while they wintered in Florida. It was finally time for us to be on our own.

I happily furnished and decorated our home, just a few miles from my parents' home and my school. There were scores of young married couples living in the development, and it wasn't long before we started making friends. I was happy, I loved David, and I loved our new life together. But I would still cry whenever we made love. Then, David would hold me and I would feel comforted, all the while thinking of my secret.

That spring, Ken put together a softball team. The young male teachers were on the team, as were the husbands of the some of the female teachers. I told David about it, and he really wanted to play. He didn't know the extent of my former relationship with Ken, and happily joined the team. We spent the entire spring and summer socializing with all the members of the softball team and their wives, and made some solid friendships. I was still nervous in Ken's company, but the discomfort was somewhat diluted by the presence of all the other couples.

I didn't know how much Ken's wife Tina knew about our relationship, but she was always warm and friendly to me. They had an adorable two-year-old little girl named Lea, and I was infatuated with her. Her giggle was infectious; she was smart and pretty. I often imagined that she was mine, or that she looked like my child, and it made my longing even greater. I would constantly ask David when we could have a baby, and he would always tell me, "I'll let you know when I'm ready."

Summer was ending, and Ken invited the whole team and their spouses to spend a weekend at his family's summer house in New Hampshire. This was the same place my parents hadn't let me visit seven years earlier. I would finally get to see what I had missed. Dare we go? David really wanted to join the group. I hadn't even told my parents that I was teaching in the same building as Ken, and certainly not that we were in the same social circle. I just told them it was the home of a friend from school, and we went. About six couples ended up going, and we had a good time hiking in the woods and enjoying the scenery. The thought persisted throughout the weekend that this life with Ken might have been mine, but it seemed like it was just a fairy tale. It was never to be.

School started again, and I was caught up in the day-to-day activities of working with 8th graders. This year I had my own classroom, so I rarely ventured out of my wing of the building. I didn't see Ken as much as I had the year before, and that was fine with me. Seeing him was too distracting.

Someone at school told me that Ken's wife Tina was pregnant again. The mere mention of the word pregnant put me in a tailspin. I was always uneasy when I heard it, as if I wore it like a scarlet letter on my chest. But this was to be Tina's second baby with Ken. I still didn't have a baby, and I wanted one so badly. I asked David again, and again his response was, "I'm not ready."

With my yearning for a child weighing on my mind, I was often depressed and angry with David. His reluctance to start a family frustrated me, and he couldn't articulate his reasons for not being "ready." On top of that, he was worried about work all the time—advertising was such a stressful business, and jobs were never stable. But we had a nice big savings account, and figured out when we would be able to afford to buy a house. The time was not far off. Maybe David was just enjoying being young and playing with his little sports car, and knew that children would change our lives forever.

Whenever we would visit his family in New York, David would suffer an upset stomach, and we were often late getting there. The pressures we were both feeling created a lot of stress on our relationship, and we decided to see a marriage counselor to help us untangle our different agendas.

After one session, the counselor told us simply, "You two need to grow up. You are both so worried about what your parents think that you are afraid to think for yourselves." That made a lot of sense, but it was easier said than done.

I saw the counselor one more time—at this session, alone. I got up the nerve to tell him my secret, and about the overwhelming guilt I felt because I hadn't ever told David. The counselor thought for a minute and then said, "Don't tell him. It would serve no purpose."

I was surprised at his dismissiveness, but it gave me the permission I needed to continue my charade. Years later, after becoming a counselor myself, I continue to be shocked at the ineptitude of that therapist. Why didn't he probe the real issues—my loss, my grief, my guilt, and how those things impacted my relationships?

One morning in the early spring I arrived at school and went into the teachers' room for my customary cup of coffee before starting the day. A number of other young teachers were there already, looking very somber. "Have you heard?" one of them asked. "Tina had her baby; it was a girl, but she has Down Syndrome." My heart dropped.

How sad and difficult for them, I thought. *All their hopes and dreams . . . What happens next?* I wondered. I ached for Ken and the anguish he must be experiencing. Then it hit me: *what if there was something wrong with MY baby? I would never know.* I was suddenly overcome with anxiety. My mind was racing, my heart was beating faster and faster, and I became dizzy. I ran into the ladies' room, splashed water on my face, and tried to regain my composure. I don't know how I got through those first few classes of the day, but when my break came, I couldn't contain myself any longer. I went to the school social worker's office, and asked if I could speak to her in confidence.

I spilled out my whole story, telling her of my fear about the health of my child. She tried to reassure me, but she was accustomed to working with children and had no experience with women in my situation. So as always, all I could do was exercise my self-control, pull myself together and get on with my life. There was nothing I could do for Ken and Tina, and there was nothing I could do for myself or my lost child. By now, our child was seven years old, and had loving parents—or so I hoped, with everything in me.

My episodes of nausea, cramps, and a racing heart continued. I learned to down bottles of Pepto Bismol and Maalox to stave off the queasiness. I saw an internist who ran test after test. Maybe it's a hiatal hernia. Maybe it's a food allergy. Maybe it's lactose intolerance . . . maybe this, maybe that . . . no answers were forthcoming.

In May of 1971, staff positions were posted for a new high school in town that would be opening in the fall. I decided that I would apply for one of those jobs. Working with Ken every day was too painful a reminder of what I had lost, and my preference had always been to work with older students who needed a caring guide through their adolescent angst. Happily, I received an offer, and was excited about teaching in the brand new school right across the street from our apartment.

I threw myself into my new assignment that fall, and thoroughly enjoyed planning civics lessons and devising new techniques for getting my teenagers thinking. It was fun to be working with lots of other young teachers, as well as having many of my old teachers become colleagues. I learned what to do, and in some cases what not to do.

For me, the best part of the job was listening to my students talk. I enjoyed the opportunity to help them work through issues, come to grips with the world they would soon be entering, and understand themselves better. I hoped that my understanding and guidance would prepare them to face the challenges ahead and enter the community as productive citizens.

David and I were becoming better adjusted to our lives together, and by the following summer, David had agreed that he was finally ready to start a family. I was ecstatic. My dreams of being a wife and mother would finally be a reality. I immediately stopped using my birth control pills, and waited excitedly to see when it would happen.

Around that time, David and I started looking for a house to purchase. We fell in love with an old stucco Tudor with turrets and a beautiful curved staircase and casement windows. When we brought my parents to see it, my father dampened our enthusiasm with a hundred reasons why we shouldn't buy it. He pointed out it was too old; it probably needed lots of repairs; the windows weren't insulated; the staircase would need to be reinforced. In our youthful naiveté and insecurity, we could never go against Dad's opinion, so we continued looking.

We finally settled on a three bedroom ranch in a neighborhood of homes that were less than ten years old. The house had a nice yard and mature trees, and was a sort of a mini-version of the house I'd grown up in. It received Dad's stamp of approval (hardwood floors, roof in good condition, move-in ready), and we bought it.

Between managing the move, decorating our new home, hanging out with friends on the weekends, and teaching every day, I was quite happy. But the yearning for a child never went away. And every March, I would still cry in the shower. Usually, I would be able to stop crying by May.

CHAPTER 16
A New Family

*N*early a year went by, and not only had I not become pregnant, but I had not had a period either. Concerned, I went back to Dr. DeVoe. She said she believed I might have an underactive thyroid, and put me on medication. "You might want to quit smoking," she suggested.

"I can't quit smoking now," I said. "I'm under so much stress. I promise you, I'll quit the minute I become pregnant."

"I'll hold you to that," she said, smiling.

In June 1973 I visited Dr. DeVoe again and she ran some tests to recheck my thyroid levels. "I'll get back to you and we'll see what to do next," she said.

The next afternoon Dr. DeVoe called. "Fran, good news," she said. "You're pregnant."

"Oh my God," I cried. "I can't believe it. I am so happy!"

"Make an appointment with me in about three weeks, and we'll check to see how you're doing."

I hung up the phone and ran to tell David. "Honey, it was the doctor on the phone. I'm pregnant!"

"Really?" he said, grinning. "That's great news!"

I was so glad David was happy, too. I ran to the pantry and took out the carton of cigarettes I kept there. "Look at this," I said. With a grand flourish, I took the whole thing and threw it into the garbage. I was determined to have a healthy baby!

I went to my parents' house to tell them the news in person. Mom was so thrilled, she was beaming; but it was my father's reaction that puzzled me. For the second time in my life, I saw my father begin to weep.

"Daddy, why are you crying? I'm so happy, and I thought you would be happy too."

"Fran, I know you want this experience, but I also know that from the time you become a parent, you will forever feel all the pain your child feels, and expose yourself to a lifetime of anguish."

Of course, intellectually, I knew that, but I thought he was overreacting. As a parent I was certainly prepared to give all my love and care to my child. I knew there would be times of pain, but I was sure the moments of joy would override any heartache I might have.

At the end of summer we received the devastating news that Grandpa Abe had terminal cancer. Doctors were trying the best they could to provide treatment, but there was little else to do but make him comfortable and wait as the disease ran its course. I spent many hours visiting him at his home, sitting by his side talking, and listening to his wonderful stories.

Before too long I began to develop the obvious look of a pregnant woman. This time there would be no hiding. This time I would buy pretty maternity clothes and be proud of my expanding waistline. By August, I couldn't fit into my regular clothes anymore, so decided I'd better tell the administration at school about my pregnancy before someone else did.

Even though school was not due to start for another few weeks, the administrative staff was already there getting schedules and room assignments ready. I was very excited that I would finally be getting my own classroom, after two years as a traveling teacher. I would be teaching my favorite classes—Problems of Democracy and Psychology—as well as Civics, and that was fine with me.

I went to see who was on duty that day, and found it was Mr. Williams, one of the four assistant principals. I was still a little nervous around him, primarily because he had been my own chemistry teacher in high school, and I hadn't done particularly well in his class. He looked up as I entered the office, and I smiled and said hello.

Without returning the smile, he said, "Hello, Mrs. Levin, what brings you here today?"

"I wanted to tell you in person, that I'm very excited about the new school year, but I thought you should know that I'm pregnant."

He raised his eyebrows and studied me. "Well, that's interesting. When are you due to deliver?"

"Probably around Christmas time," I said.

"Do you really think you should be around adolescents in your condition?" he asked.

I was flabbergasted! Did he really think that teenagers didn't know where babies came from? Maybe he thought that was the problem—they DID know where babies come from, and they shouldn't be thinking about those things.

"And are you healthy enough to be working?" he queried.

"I'm absolutely healthy," I asserted.

"Well," he said, "you should probably plan to leave by Thanksgiving."

This was not the conversation I was expecting. How could he decide when I should leave? I was planning to work up until Christmas vacation began, or until I had the baby, whatever came first.

"We'll see," I declared. I left the building more than a little dispirited, wondering if he could really force me to leave before I wanted to. However, I spent the remaining weeks of summer with my friends, enjoying the beach, shopping, and planning the décor of the baby's room in our new house.

Finally, the end of summer vacation came, and with it the first few days of teacher preparation for the new school year. As the teachers assembled excitedly in planning meetings, we all received our schedules and opening day instructions.

I was shocked to see that my schedule contained a multitude of classrooms. The room that was to have been mine had been given to another teacher, and my schedule had been totally changed from what it had been when I left.

"What happened to my schedule?" I heatedly asked my department head.

"Well," he said. "Mr. Williams decided that since you wouldn't be here all year, it didn't make sense to give you your own room. And, since Mrs. Jayne was planning to come back second semester anyway from her medical leave, she can just take over your schedule when you leave."

"What about all my materials? I'll have to lug everything with me from class to class again? I'll be going up and down stairs, from one end of the building to the other!"

But despite my objections, my room assignment was not changed back. However, I was determined to make it work, if for no other reason than to show Mr. Williams he couldn't dispense with me so easily.

So, for the first few weeks of classes, I trudged up and down the stairs carrying all my materials. If I had AV equipment or extensive materials, I'd take the elevator, but otherwise, I hiked from room to room. By October I was a wreck, coming home from school in the afternoons totally exhausted. While I still loved teaching, it seemed so unfair that Mr. Williams would make it harder for me in my pregnant condition.

In desperation, I called my union representative. "Can they really do that to me?" I asked. "They changed my entire schedule and made it virtually impossible for me. It's even more challenging than my first two years of being a traveling teacher. And how can he decide when I should leave? And how does he get to tell me I won't be back second semester? I never told him I wouldn't."

"Well," he said. "You have several choices. You can file a grievance and then go to back and forth to Hartford when the hearings begin. Or, you can take all your sick days and get them to hire a substitute for you now. Then you wouldn't be running all over the building, and you would still be getting paid."

"I'll think about it," I said. What they were doing to me was so wrong, but that was what they did to pregnant women at that time. They wanted us to stay home where we "belonged," and not be front and center for the world to ogle—especially impressionable teenagers. Life hadn't changed much since the 1950's after all.

I discussed my problem with David. I knew that in my eighth month I would be in no shape to fight anyone, especially since my teachers' union wasn't up for the fight either.

Reluctantly, I decided to follow the union rep's advice and use all my sick days—my sixty-plus days would get me to Christmas vacation.

Staying home and not working was a new experience for me. I spent my days productively—decorating the baby's room, baking and cooking, doing volunteer work, and spending time with friends who were home with their young children.

By now, Grandpa Abe had been hospitalized, and I visited him almost every day to bring whatever happiness and comfort I could to his days.

Before I knew it, Christmas had come—and still no baby.

Dr. DeVoe was seeing me weekly by then. She said the baby was doing fine, but the little one wasn't ready to come yet. The New Year 1974 came, and still no baby. My phone rang constantly with friends and family seeking updates. I had nothing to tell them. I wondered if my body was somehow holding on to this baby, afraid of another traumatic loss.

Finally, at the end of the first week in January, Dr. DeVoe agreed that some action might need to be taken.

"Since we don't know exactly when you conceived, it's hard to say if the baby is really late. We won't know until you deliver." She described what a post-mature baby would look like, and then she said, "Let's give it the weekend. Everything still looks good. If you don't deliver by Monday, you can come into the office, and there is a procedure I can do that may help push things along."

On Monday, when I still hadn't delivered, I called her.

"Okay, come into the office tomorrow morning, and we'll see what we can do."

So, on Tuesday morning, I plodded back into the doctor's office, hoping that she could do something. As she examined me once again, she did some internal manipulation, and told me I would probably go into labor soon.

I left to go a friend's house for lunch, and less than two hours later, as I was sitting at her kitchen table, I began to feel cramping.

This is it, I thought. I told my friend what was happening, and drove the few blocks home. I called David and told him I was in labor. "Hurry home, we need to get ready."

I phoned the doctor and told her about the magic she had performed. I could almost see her smiling on the other end of the phone. She told me how to time my contractions and when I should plan to go to the hospital. She told me if I could hold off until midnight we wouldn't have to pay the extra day at the hospital!

David sat by my side, keeping me company and timing every twinge. Finally, we drove to the hospital, eager with anticipation. I didn't care about the pain, I only wanted to hold my baby.

At three-thirty Wednesday morning, January 9, with David holding my hands, I gave birth to a baby boy. He was a healthy seven pounds six ounces, with red, patchy skin and a full head of dark hair. I fell in love instantly. David was ecstatic. We had a son! Dr. DeVoe said that the condition of his skin was a pretty good indication that he was a bit post-mature, but that extra time had given him some extra weight, and that was a good thing.

David and I called our parents with the good news, and just before dawn, I was wheeled down to my hospital room, tired, but happy. Through the window, I saw a light snow had begun to fall, and all seemed right with the world.

My first baby is almost ten years old, I thought. Tears of both joy and sadness dripped from my eyes.

We decided to name our new baby Corey Scott—Corey, in memory of Grandma Ceil, and Scott for my great-grandmother Sophie.

The following Sunday, Corey and I were released from the hospital. "David, please let's stop at Grandpa Abe's house on the way home so he can see the baby." Grandpa had been released from the hospital several weeks earlier to spend his last days in the comfort of his home. I knew he was usually unresponsive lately, but I still had to do this.

"Of course, Fran. I know how much it means to you," he replied.

We quietly entered the house. A hospital bed had been set up in the living room, and a nurse and Grandma Esther sat in the chairs pulled up around it.

"Grandpa," I whispered. "There's someone here to meet you." I held the baby tightly in my arms and sat down at the edge of the bed.

"Grandpa, this is your great-grandson, Corey Scott." I touched Grandpa's hand with my own, and felt the warmth radiating from it. His eyelids fluttered, and he took a breath. I sat for another minute or two, put his hand on the baby, and said, "Sweet dreams, Grandpa." In my heart I knew he was aware of our presence.

David helped me to my feet. "I'd better get these two home," he said. "I'm sure they are both very tired."

The next morning, Mom came to the house. "Daddy couldn't come with me," she said. "He went to Grandpa's."

Mom prepared a little breakfast for me, and we made plans for Corey's bris that was to be held at our home on Wednesday.

Shortly after noon the phone rang. It was Dad. "Grandpa's gone," he said. "He died a little while ago. I was able to make arrangements to have the funeral tomorrow."

I thought of the wonderful man my grandfather was, and what a huge loss his passing was to our family.

A twinge of guilt ran through me as I remembered how dishonest we had been with him about my reasons for going away. I could only imagine how much making the decision to withhold the truth from him must have hurt my father. Overwhelmed, once again, with guilt at the rift I caused in my family, my tears fell. I cried for all my losses and let myself feel the pain.

David and I worked out a routine for caring for our baby. When Corey woke during the night, David would get up, change his diapers, and bring him to me so I could nurse him.

Holding my newborn son was the most comforting thing I had ever experienced. The joy at nursing him and providing him with love and sustenance was miraculous.

When the morning of the funeral came, I was a jumble of emotions as I prepared to say goodbye to my grandfather for the last time. I had given birth only six days earlier, and I dressed in one of the few dresses I had that fit me. I applied my make-up with care, hoping to look as good as I could for all the relatives who would be there. My dear friend Nadine came to stay with Corey during the time I would be out of the house, and I carefully timed my departure around Corey's feeding schedule. Despite my grief, I found the Jewish funeral rituals to be familiar and soothing. After the funeral we hurried back to the comfort of our home and our new baby.

Wednesday morning we got up early to get ready for Corey's bris. I had arranged to have the food delivered, and all Mom had to do was help me set everything out. The rest would be taken care of by my friends and other family.

After we had greeted all the guests, the rabbi suggested I retire to my bedroom, nurse Corey, and rest for a while. Nancy followed me into the room, and sat on my bed as I fed my baby. She looked at me empathically and said, "I know what you're thinking, Fran."

I nodded as a tear rolled down my cheek. It was just like Nancy to be in tune with my emotions and thoughts. She was indeed the trusted friend I had always thought her to be.

When David knocked on the door to retrieve our son for the ceremony, I smiled at him and Nan squeezed my hand.

After the bris, the days flew by, and Corey became the center of my existence. Before long, he was returning my gaze, smiling, playing, and turning into a toddler. He began talking before he could even walk, and was totally enthralled with his toys and books. My friend Nadine gave birth to a daughter just three months after I had Corey, and we spent countless hours going on field trips to greenhouses and zoos, and lunching and shopping together.

On the days we weren't driving around, we would put the children in a playpen together, drink coffee and share stories of our lives. But as close as Nadine and I became, never once was I brave enough to tell her my true story. That Fran was still buried so deeply, I was afraid to show who I really was for fear I would lose everything.

When Corey was just three months old, David lost his job. After three months of finding nothing nearby, he was offered a position with an advertising agency in Miami. We knew we had to move. While it was difficult leaving our home and our families, I chose to view it as an adventure. It would be a chance for us to forge our independence.

The year was 1974 and the country was suffering through a serious recession. Mortgage interest rates were astronomical, but we put our house on the market and crossed our fingers.

In early July, we packed our belongings and made the move to Florida. David had found us a cute two bedroom apartment near the University of Miami, and I had no trouble unpacking and making it ours. I would drive David to work every day, then spend the rest of my time exploring. I reached out to the daughter of one of Mom's friends, who lived just a few miles from us, and started to meet other young women. Our social life began to grow.

David seemed to enjoy his job at the agency, but one day in October he came home ashen-faced. His employer had let him go. Apparently, the clearances for a particular photo shoot had gone awry, and he was the one who had to take the fall. We were devastated, but eventually I began to see it as another opportunity. Our house in Connecticut had never sold; we could move back into it as if we had never left, and David could continue looking for a job closer to home.

We rented a truck so David could drive back with our belongings, and I drove our car with Corey in his car seat in the back.

The trip took several days, and late in the afternoon on the second day I began feeling nauseated. I hated the thought of being sick, and pulled over to the side of the road to get a grip on myself. My heart began to beat faster, I started to sweat, and my stomach rolled over. The familiar symptoms, which usually came at night, were now appearing during the day! *What was happening to me?* I took a sip of water, then a deep breath, and tried to settle myself. After a half hour or so, I began to feel a little better, and continued driving until we stopped for the evening.

My sleep that night was restless, and I dreamed a dream I'd had many times before. In the nightmare, I lost Corey, and couldn't find him anywhere. David woke me and told me I was crying out in my sleep. I let him hold me and tell me it was okay—Corey was just fine, and in his port-a-crib, just a few feet away.

We called that time in Florida our "vacation with the furniture," and were home by Halloween. It took David another couple of months to find a job, but with that and my parents' help, soon we were back on our feet.

Even before Corey was two, I knew I wanted another child. Being a mother was the most satisfying thing I had ever done, and I needed to prove to myself that I was a good one. I became pregnant very quickly this time. Although I didn't gain much weight, my new obstetrician, Dr. Binder, reassured me everything was fine. I felt much better physically than I had when I was pregnant with Corey, and continued my busy schedule of caring for my active toddler, going to charity meetings, and enjoying bowling and tennis with my friends.

I went into labor on the escalator at Bloomingdales. Nadine and I were there one evening to do some last-minute shopping, and as we were about to leave, I felt a twinge. It wasn't particularly painful, and I playfully suggested we stop for ice cream. By the time I got home, I realized that this was the real thing, and started timing my contractions.

Jason Adam was born at one-thirty in the morning on October 1, and I was beyond ecstatic. He looked so different from Corey. While Corey had a full head of dark hair, hazel eyes, and was red and wrinkled when he was born, Jason was fair and had only a wisp of blonde hair. His skin was clear and silky, and his eyes large, round and blue.

Again we held the ritual bris, and we celebrated with our friends and family. I felt far less melancholy this time. I was the mother of two boys, and I relished my role of being a wife and homemaker. It was my dream come true—the picture I'd always had of myself. I could tell myself and show the world my perfect family, and I was the only one who knew what was in my heart. I learned that if you tell yourself something often enough, you can almost make it true. There were times when I forgot about the pain, forgot about my dishonesty, and lived solely in the moment.

Inevitably, though, spring would come again, and I would spend hours crying—always in the shower, so David wouldn't know.

Corey demanded the bulk of my attention, while Jason was an easy baby who rarely cried. He ate and slept well, and acclimated easily to being toted around on errands. It wasn't much more work caring for the two boys than it had been with one. I felt myself yearning for another child. Now that I had two boys, it was time for me to have a daughter. Having grown up with only a sister, I hadn't known much about little boys, and what I didn't know, I had learned. How hard could another child be?

I got a book from a friend on "choosing the sex of your baby," and we started trying to conceive a girl. Unfortunately, month after month, I didn't become pregnant. I was beginning to worry. Was something wrong with me or David?

I conferred with Dr. Binder, and he told me to stop worrying—it had only been a few months. "Get rid of that book," he said.

So, I tossed the book and figured we would take our chances. Miraculously, I became pregnant the very next month! We excitedly planned for the birth of our third child.

David, a talented woodworker, made bunk beds and bookcases for the boys, and we turned our den into a new nursery. Between activities with the children and my housework, the days passed quickly. I did everything I could to become the perfect wife and mother. My volunteer work became very important to me, and after several years of serving as vice president of a local chapter of ORT, an organization devoted to providing training programs and building schools, I became its president. My confidence in myself grew with every challenge, and most of the time I was pleased with my life.

From time to time I would have a dream in which the high school administration discovered I hadn't ever graduated because in the year I was gone, I hadn't satisfied the foreign language requirement. They had mistakenly allowed me to go to college, and I worried that all the hard work I had done would be negated. My lies caught up with me, even in my sleep.

On a Sunday morning in August, after a light breakfast, I began my labor. It came on quickly, while I was in the shower, and my parents rushed over to watch the boys. David and I sped to the hospital, and upon our arrival, Dr. Binder's partner, Dr. Lewis, greeted us. He checked on me and told me it would be hours yet, and said he was going to go home and would return later. What he hadn't counted on was my determination, and my body's will to have this child.

Even before Dr. Lewis returned, I was ready to deliver. The nurses implored me to wait, and I couldn't help but smile as I watched him running down the hall, putting on his gloves and mask. One of the nurses said to me, "Don't push yet, you have to wait until we get you into the delivery room!"

My logical thinking prevailed. I was going to have this baby, boy or girl, on MY terms, even if it was in the hallway. I was in a hospital, my baby was ready to be born, and I pushed. I kept thinking of the TV show, *My Three Sons.* If I wasn't blessed with a daughter, I was going to have a household full of rumble tumble boys, like the charming TV family.

There in the hallway, I gave birth to a perfect baby girl. Maybe there was a God who was smiling down on me. Maybe I had redeemed myself. Alexis Kate was like a tiny doll. She had tufts of dark hair, an angelic little mouth, and the tiniest fingers and toes I had ever seen.

My family was complete—almost. I had three of the most beautiful children anyone could ask for. I loved my husband, my home, and my life. But the nagging pain in my heart never went away. Where is my lost child? He or she is fifteen years old now. What does she look like? What sports does he play? Is she good in school? Do his parents love him the way I would have? Not a day went by when I didn't ask myself those questions. Yet I had three children and a husband at home who needed me to be there for them. I could only hope and pray that my first child's parents were there for him or her.

CHAPTER 17
Life Changes

*T*he years sped by so quickly, many memories elude me, even now. My children thrived and grew. I had solid friendships and a comfortable marriage. David and I had our ups and downs, mainly due to his frequent job changes, yet we always seemed to manage—often assisted by my parents, who loved me and my children to the core. When we argued, it was always about one of two things—the children or money.

When we argued about the children, it was always over the same issue: I needed a compelling reason if I was going to discipline them. My parenting style was in part a reaction to the kind of parenting I had received, as well as a desire to apply what I had learned when studying child development. I wanted to be the kind of parent who loved her children unconditionally. I wanted them to know that whatever happened or whatever they did, I would always be there for them. My parents had never used physical discipline on me, and I didn't believe it was necessary.

David, on the other hand, grew up in a family where discipline came first and he was not to question authority. His father frequently "got out the belt," and there were no opportunities for discussion. David maintained that when it came to the children, they should just listen to him because he was their father. Often, when they would question his decisions, he would reply, "Because I said so." We would frequently discuss this, and it made no sense to me. But nothing I said to him could change his mind.

The children eventually learned which parent to go to for the answers they wanted. David believed I let them walk all over me, and I believed that he closed down dialog. We were polar opposites in our parenting, and in retrospect I think we might have served our children better had we both been more moderate.

Jason, Alexis, and Corey, 1981.

As to our finances, when we had enough money, everything was fine, but during the times David was unemployed, things were not so fine. Unfortunately, he continued to spend money like we still had it, and finally, when Alexis was only two, I had to go back to work. I resented it terribly. Most of my friends were still able to stay at home with their children, and I hated putting my little girl in day care. It broke my heart to do it, but I had no choice.

I found a job as the office assistant in a social service agency that did case management for abused and neglected children. Part of my responsibility was to organize and maintain its library, and I learned a great deal during my years there. Eventually, I moved to another agency, running a mentoring program for children who were between ages six and twelve. Usually they were kids in single parent homes, and I managed and grew the program enthusiastically. My heart went out to the parents, and I taught them parenting skills. I also helped the program's mentors to find a balance between being a friend to the children and becoming over-involved in their problems.

In addition to working at these jobs, I would still do charitable work and volunteer in the children's schools whenever I could. In 1984, David's father died. It was the first time either of us had to deal with handling the death of a parent.

When I married David, I had decided that I would be the best daughter-in-law ever, and I had made good on that promise to myself. David's mother was emotionally unprepared to be a widow. While she was certainly competent to take care of the details of everyday living, her depression was immobilizing. Several times a month she would come from New York and stay with us, enjoying the company and support we offered. We found that during these visits, she was a big help around the house. She and I got along fine, and David and I discussed the idea of her coming to live with us. If she gave up her New York apartment, we could look for a larger home and she could contribute to the mortgage. It seemed like it would be a good arrangement for us all.

In the spring of 1986 we moved to our dream home. It was a two story expanded Cape Cod style in an established neighborhood with large yards and mature landscaping. I had loved that area of Norwalk my whole life. Best of all, the children could remain in the schools they were in, so the transition would be an easy one.

The house had three bedrooms upstairs, so the children all had rooms of their own. The ground level had a huge master bedroom and bath, an office, a powder room, a beautiful sun-lit living room, an eat-in kitchen with lots of storage, and an enormous loft over the garage, which we made into a studio for my mother-in-law. The home was situated on over an acre of verdant property, punctuated by a running brook and a wonderful yard that could host a beautiful garden.

I was filled with so much hope and excitement for our lives in that house. The day of the closing, I went back to the house alone, while David supervised the movers at our old house. I sat on the hearth of the fireplace, looked up at the cathedral ceiling, and thought that life couldn't get much better. We were going to be living in the kind of home we'd always coveted, our children would thrive here, and if I had to sacrifice a vacation or two in order to afford it, I could easily live with that.

For a while, things were as perfect as I had imagined. I excitedly planned Corey's Bar Mitzvah for the following January. That event too was perfect. I was so proud of him, and the celebration party could not have gone more smoothly. My life was just as I had imagined when I was young—I had a home of my own, a loving husband who adored me, and beautiful, smart children. I was playing the role of the perfect wife, mother, daughter, friend, and sister.

But late at night when I couldn't sleep, when I would writhe with nausea, and every spring when I would slip into weeks of depression—those were the times I knew what an imposter I was.

In the late fall of 1988, Dad was having symptoms that necessitated an angioplasty. He was admitted to the hospital and had numerous tests before and after the procedure. Doctors assured him the procedure would help prevent a heart attack. Unfortunately, some of the X-rays showed a spot on his lung, so he scheduled consultations with an oncologist.

Wednesday, December 21, 1988 was our nineteenth wedding anniversary. That night the news was filled with the traumatic news of Pan American Flight 103 being sabotaged by a bomb and going down over Lockerbie, Scotland, killing two hundred seventy people. The scope of the tragedy made a deep impression on me. Stories of the lives of those killed resonated with me. These were parents, children, husbands and wives. For weeks I wondered about the safety of my lost child, now a twenty-five-year-old adult. If some tragedy had befallen him or her, how would I ever know? The not knowing gnawed at me constantly.

After the angioplasty, Dad's oncologist determined that he would need surgery. Slightly more than three months later, on my forty-third birthday, I sat in the surgical waiting room with my mother. After interminable hours, the surgeon came into the room. He was beaming. "We got it all," he said. "I'm sure he will be just fine."

Mom and I were greatly relieved, and within a week, she was able to take him home to recover in comfort. But as the weeks passed, Dad had a hard time healing. Fluid accumulated in his lungs, and he developed a cough and unrelenting pain. He returned to the doctor again and again. Then he was readmitted to the hospital.

We learned that the cancer had metastasized throughout his body. From the surgery, cancer cells had been released to flow through his bloodstream, and he declined rapidly.

Sidra, who had a baby and a toddler at home in Boston, came to stay for as long as she could. It was hard for her, living three hours away. She was torn between wanting to spend quality time with our father, and wanting to be with her young family who needed her so much. She finally said her goodbyes and returned sadly to Boston.

I visited Dad in the hospital every day. One Friday in mid-June, he seemed so much better. When I arrived after work, he was sitting up in a chair, and he and Mom told me he had agreed to start chemotherapy the next day.

Then his tone shifted. "Your mother and I want you to know something. We are proud of the woman you have become," he started. "We forgive you for what happened in the past, and sincerely want you to know that."

I felt lightheaded. They have forgiven my sin? I have redeemed myself in their eyes? What were the implications of that? Could I now begin to forgive myself? It would take a while to process this.

"I'm sorry I put you through that," I said somberly, as I welled up with tears.

"We just wanted you to know," Dad repeated.

"Thank you for everything you have done for me, I know you have always had my best interests at heart. I love you," I assured them.

When I returned to the hospital the next afternoon, Dad was sleeping deeply. Mom shook her head, and shared with me the details of the doctor's visit that morning. He had told her it was useless to begin the chemotherapy.

I called David and asked him to come and bring the children to say goodbye to their grandfather. It was so hard for me to watch them tearfully whispering to their Poppi, who remained unresponsive.

When they left, Mom and I flipped around the channels on the TV, and I told her I would stay with her as long as I could. The nurses intermittently flitted in and out, checking Dad's vital signs and changing his IV drip. I found a TV station that was playing one of my favorite movies, Carousel, and it made the time go more quickly. Mom and I sang along to the familiar music, and spoke quietly during the commercials.

I noticed that Dad's breathing had become slower and slower. At about eleven o'clock in the evening, when I looked over at him, I realized he was not breathing at all. I ran out to the desk and called the nurse. She quickly followed me back into the room. After giving him a short examination, she looked up. "He's gone," she said compassionately.

The next few hours were marked by bursts of activity punctuated by tearful silences and reflection. A doctor on duty came into the room to do the final pronouncements, and I asked a nurse what the process would be. She explained that the hospital would make contact with the funeral home, and that we should call our rabbi in the morning. She said it would be a while before the staff from the morgue came to get him, so we could sit with him until then to say our goodbyes.

Finally, the time came, and faced with the empty room, we had nothing to do but leave the hospital for the last time. We solemnly left the hospital and realized it was Sunday morning—Fathers' Day.

Neither Mom nor I slept much, and so by seven o' clock we were ready to begin making phone calls. I ran home to shower and change my clothes. I grabbed my address book, and then called our rabbi. He said he would meet us Monday morning at my parents' home.

I gathered my children close to me and told them what to expect over the next few days, and was comforted by their affection and reflections. Because they were so close to their grandfather, I knew their own grief would be difficult for them, so I made sure they each had a voice and a role to play if they chose to do so.

Sidra and her family arrived the next day, and we talked about how we wanted Dad's service to be. We both sat down and began to write our individual eulogies. Clearly I was sad to have lost my father; I was sad he wouldn't see my children grow up, and sad we would never again be able to share the hours talking and philosophizing together.

When the rabbi came, he asked all of us what special memories we had of Dad, what stories he might share, and about the kind of person he was. Silently, I thought of many stories and moments I would never be able to share with anyone. Something shifted inside of me, and another piece of my heart withered.

The funeral was scheduled for Tuesday morning. Everyone had been notified. There was nothing left to do but examine my feelings. I read through copies of Elizabeth Kubler-Ross' book, *On Death and Dying* as well as Harold Kushner's book, *When Bad Things Happen to Good People.* I read books on Jewish tradition and how members of my faith created rituals to help the grieving. Then I went back to trying to write my eulogy. The words wouldn't come. That shattered part of my soul had been denied words for twenty-five years, and when I called for them, they still would not come.

I sat with Sidra and told her that I was not up to the task of giving Dad's memorial tribute. We had shared the stories, shared the reminiscences. Now I asked her to please speak the words I could not. I was not ready to say goodbye to my father for the last time. I didn't know it then, but I still had unfinished business with him.

In August, my mother-in-law discovered that she was in urgent need of a heart valve replacement. She scheduled it as soon as she could, so I made plans to take some time off from work to care for her when she got home. She tried to laugh it off, but we knew what a big deal open heart surgery is, and it was very stressful for us all.

When the children returned to school in September, we often had to remind them that their grandmother was right upstairs recuperating, and they needed to be quiet so she could rest. Tell that to three kids between ten and fifteen!

Ultimately, in September, I resumed work at my job at the agency, and at the same time was assigned to a big new office with a roommate. Alice and I both had our own phones and desks, and when we needed to do private interviews, there was always a free space we could use to take care of that.

There was, however, no avoiding hearing Alice talking on the phone to her clients. She worked for the adoption department of the agency, and her responsibility was to counsel prospective birth parents and adoptive parents. I sometimes asked her questions about the feelings and circumstances of her clients, and I went home every night thinking about how I had never received any kind of counseling prior to or after the relinquishment of my baby.

So much had changed in twenty-five years. Still, I didn't share with anyone what had happened to me. To do so would be to betray my family and admit to the lie I had perpetuated for so many years.

October 14, the day of Jay's Bar Mitzvah, was a beautiful autumn gold day, and the leaves were at high peak. As we celebrated Jay's entry into the adult life of our religious congregation, my father's absence was palpable. Jason affectionately paid homage to him in his speech to the congregation.

Overall, the merriment of our friends and family, the dancing and singing, and the spirit of the baseball-themed party all contributed to making the day nearly perfect. But in the midst of preparations and at times that day, I felt twinges of guilt, because with my father's death had come a kind of liberation. I no longer had to worry about making any decision that he would judge. It dawned on me that whatever I chose to do for that party, for my family, or just for me would be okay.

Three days later, I was cleaning up from dinner, and David settled into the family room to watch TV. Game three of the World Series was about to begin, and announcers had started their commentary.

About ten past eight, David called me into the room. "They just had a big earthquake in San Francisco," he shouted. With that, the news broke into the regularly scheduled broadcasting. We learned that the game had been postponed, and for the next few hours, the broadcast brought stories of devastation. The quake had been measured at a magnitude of 6.9, and was responsible for numerous road and building collapses. Over sixty people died, and more than thirty-five hundred suffered injury.

How many young adults migrate to California from Arizona? I wondered. *Could my child have been there and suffered injury or worse?* I could not get the thoughts out of my head.

I immediately lost my appetite. I couldn't think of anything but my lost child. Once again, the worry and fear began to overtake me. It was all I could do to hold myself together.

CHAPTER 18

A New Journey Begins

*P*art of my job involved going to visit my students and their teachers at school, as well as at their homes. For the older children, I'd communicate with their school counselors to make sure the mentors had access to them there, and to be better able to share information with them as to their adjustment and involvement in our program.

In early November, I made a visit to one of the middle schools where my client's counselor was my own former third grade teacher, Louise Roman. She was a vibrant, caring woman who remembered me as one of her more active students. She'd had contact with my mother over the years because her children had been in my mother's class at the school where Mom taught. *What a small world,* I thought.

Little did I know how small it was! I walked into the building and went to the main office. Greeting visitors at the front desk was the assistant principal—Ken Jamison. I hadn't seen Ken in 16 years. I don't know which of us was more shocked to see the other, yet he kept his cool and welcomed me warmly.

"I'm here to see Louise Roman," I said. "She works with several students who are in my mentoring program." I hoped he couldn't read in my face the jumble of emotions I was feeling at the sight of him.

"Fine, I'll bring you to her office. It's right down the hall." He smiled at me, and my heart beat faster. "When you're done with her, come see me. I'd love to hear what you've been up to."

Louise greeted me affectionately. "You know Ken?" she inquired. "Yes, I've known him forever. He was my boyfriend in high school, and we worked together a long time ago. But we haven't seen each other since I left Western Middle School."

"What a coincidence," she replied. I pondered all the coincidences in my life . . . I would think more about that at another time. For the next half hour we spoke about her students and my mentoring program; then it was time to leave. I walked out the door, and Ken was standing in the door of his office talking to someone.

He looked over at me. "Come on in, Fran. It's so good to see you."

I followed him into his office, and he asked me about my family and about my work. When I told him how much I enjoyed working with the children, and how much I missed teaching, he thought for a moment and then said, "You know, Louise has taught me a lot about counseling. I think you'd make a great counselor."

"I took an elective grad school course, *Intro to Counseling*, and I really liked it," I told him. "Maybe I'll look into it."

My brain was running a hundred miles an hour. *He thinks I'd make a good counselor? He actually is thinking about that? I'm in his consciousness?*

"Tell me about your family," I said. "How's Tina? And your kids?" He filled me in on his full life, and asked me about mine. We chatted about the things in our life that were most important, as well as things that were mundane—the music we liked, when we did our best thinking, what we did for fun. Finally, it was time for me to leave.

"I really enjoyed seeing you," I said. He smiled genially.

"It was great seeing you too," he affirmed. "Take care of yourself."

I left the building and sat in my car. I couldn't move. A wave of sadness came over me, and I put my head down on the steering wheel and let the tears come. I had sat across from Ken for the better part of an hour—and was unable to say the words that I had wanted to tell him for twenty-five years.

There hadn't been even one day since last March that I hadn't cried. This year I hadn't been able to wrap my sorrow in a tidy package, tie it with a ribbon and put it away. Not a moment went by when thoughts of Ken and our child hadn't permeated my every waking hour. At night, I tossed and turned, unable to find rest. When I did sleep, it was fitful. I had no appetite. My clothes were all too big, and I discovered that I had lost more than twenty-five pounds. I'd been sad before, but never like this. I knew, from what I had learned working at the agency, that I was in trouble.

But whom could I trust? Who would understand and point me in the right direction? I couldn't tell David or any of my friends. They would all think less of me. David would be angry at my betrayal, and my friends would all try to minimize what I was feeling—if I could even get past the shame of it all.

It finally dawned on me—Faith, the director of the agency where I worked, would understand. She was a social worker. Wasn't it her job to understand? After days of battling with myself, I was more afraid of not sharing this than I was of being found out. I had no choice. I made an appointment to see her, and when it was time, I warily walked into her office.

"Faith, I need your help," I started. "I have no one else to turn to, and I can't go on like this any longer."

Through tears and sobs, I told her my story. I told her about my parents forcing me to break up with Ken, about finding out I was pregnant, about being sent away. I told her I had no choice about giving up my baby, and I told her of the years of wondering, of guilt, of lying and self-loathing, of trying to be perfect to atone for my sins.

She listened patiently, and when I was finished, she gazed over at me and said, "Fran, I am so sorry for what you went through. I will do whatever I can to help you."

"Is there a social worker—not someone here—you can recommend?" I pleaded.

"I know just the person," she said. "She has extensive experience, and I respect her without reservation. I know you will love her, and I trust she'll be able to help you."

"Thank you so much," I wept.

I took the phone number she offered me, and returned to my office. Blessedly, Alice wasn't there. I wouldn't have to make any explanations or be overheard on the phone. I looked down at the paper in my hand. "Eleanor Green," it said, along with her phone number. With my heart beating faster, I dialed. To my disappointment, I connected with an answering machine.

I left her a message about Faith's recommendation, and gave my name and my work phone number, stating I would be there for a few more hours. I waited apprehensively. Could this woman really help me?

Less than an hour later, the phone rang. I told Eleanor the urgency of my situation, and she was able to see me within the next few days.

That night, I told David about my depression. I told him about my lack of appetite, my weight loss, my overriding sadness. I told him I made an appointment to get help. He was extremely supportive, and encouraged me to do whatever was necessary to feel better.

The next Saturday morning, I drove nervously to Eleanor's office. It was in a charming old house which had been converted into three offices upstairs. I climbed the steep flight of stairs and found a tiny vestibule with one chair. I heard quiet murmurs coming from behind one of the doors. I sat impatiently in the chair, thumbed through some magazines on the table nearby, and waited. My heart was pounding with anxiety and my brain wasn't registering anything from the written pages before me.

Finally, the door opened, and a lovely woman with beautiful reddish hair, milky white skin, and a smile in her eyes poked her head out.

"Fran?" she queried.

"Yes," I answered timidly.

"Please come in," she welcomed.

Her tiny office contained her office chair as well as a big easy chair, a desk and another chair, and a work nook with bookcases. It was simple, yet warm and welcoming. I chose to sit in the easy chair directly across from her while she took down my basic information.

"How can I help you?" she asked.

My story came spilling out. I told her, as I had told Faith, the story of my losses, of love that never had a chance to run its course and of my surrendered child. I described my physical ailments, which I had by now realized were in reality crushing anxiety attacks, and of the secrets, lies, and shame I had carried with me for so long.

An hour later, I left her office with another appointment made, and the hope that my burdens would somehow find a way to be lifted.

I decided to drive a bit more before I went home. I needed to think, to allow myself to feel, and to analyze the words Eleanor and I had spoken.

The woods were nearly finished shedding their autumn colors, but as I drove, I felt a sense of relief.

Before long I found myself at the reservoir Ken and I had frequented so many years before. I parked my car in the familiar spot and got out, taking in the smells of the forest and its blessed quiet.

I wonder if our tree is still here, I thought. I walked down the path and looked around. Twenty-five years is a long time. Trees die; new trees grow. The path down to the water hadn't changed at all. I slowly traversed the incline, looking up at the evergreen canopy.

When the vastness of the water opened up before me, I sat on one of the huge boulders and reflected on the vista's consistency. So much had changed in my life, and undoubtedly in Ken's, but our place was still here, and would be forever. And somewhere else was a part of both of us—a living, breathing young adult—who didn't know who we were, or how much he or she was cherished.

It was time for me to leave. I continued to look for that special tree, but couldn't find it. It didn't really matter; this beautiful place would always be in my heart.

By Monday, I had made some decisions. In case our child was looking for us, I had to set the record straight. I had to amend the records to reflect our correct names. It was really all about making sure that his or her right to know the truth was honored. It was the least I could do.

What did I remember? I remembered the agency, the hospital, the doctor. I called information to get the phone number of the Arizona Children's Home. They were the guardians of the adoption records, so I would start there.

Late Tuesday morning, I nervously picked up the phone and dialed. A friendly voice at the other end asked how she could help.

"I relinquished a baby there in 1964, and I want to provide some information to the record," I stated.

"Let me put you in touch with a social worker," she said. "She'll be happy to help you."

"Good Morning, this is Marsha. How can I help you?"

"Hi Marsha, my name is Fran, and I gave up a baby there in March of 1964. I gave some wrong information that I would like to correct."

"OK," she said without judgment. "I can help you with that. Let me get some information from you."

She proceeded to ask me simple things like my current name and address, and the date of the baby's birth. Then she inquired, "What was the sex of the baby?"

"I don't know," I answered. "No one ever told me. They said it would be easier for me if I didn't know."

"Things were so different then," she responded. "Let me see if I can locate your file. Can I call you back in about an hour?"

"Of course, I'll be at my desk," I replied. The next hour dragged by without a call, but finally, about ninety minutes later, the phone rang.

"Good afternoon, this is Fran," I answered.

"Hi Fran, this is Marsha . . . Congratulations, you have a girl."

"Oh my God! I thought . . . I wondered . . . that is wonderful. Thank you so much for telling me."

"I thought it was important for you to know—I'm going to send you a letter in the mail with a release form attached. You can make the changes on there and get it back to me. There is a small charge for the service. Fran, have you gone for any help with this—emotionally, I mean?"

"I just started seeing a therapist," I told her.

"There are support groups for this that can help you, too," she offered.

"Really? I wouldn't know how to go about finding one."

"I might be able to get you the information. Hold on a minute." Before I knew it she was back on the line. "Here you go," she said. "There is a group in Stratford, Connecticut. Is that near you?"

"Yes, about twenty minutes!" I was incredulous.

"Great. It's called Ties That Bind. The leader's name is Jane. I'll give you her phone number."

"Thank you so much, Marsha. I'll be looking for your letter." I hung up the phone and took a deep breath.

CHAPTER 19
Disclosure

*T*he following Sunday afternoon was gray and blustery—a typical wet New England December day. I told David I was going to a support group meeting recommended by my therapist, Eleanor. While I still hadn't told him the whole truth, I had at least let him know I was depressed and seeking help.

I pulled my coat closer around me as I entered the supermarket and looked for the staircase that would take me to the meeting room. There it was—behind the floral department. *How fitting*, I thought—*how funereal*.

I cautiously climbed the stairs, not knowing what I would find behind the meeting room door. What would they look like? Would they be trampy looking women with too much makeup? Would they be naïve and pasty-faced? Where would I fit in?

I warily opened the door and saw a large table filled with about a dozen women who greeted me enthusiastically.

"I . . . I talked to Jane about the meeting here?" I asked.

"I'm Jane," a kind woman spoke up. "Please join us."

I looked around the room and saw plain faces, pretty faces, faces you'd smile at as you were walking down the street.

"This is how it works," Jane began. "We go around the table, and each woman can say whatever she wants, or simply pass. You can tell your story, ask for feedback, or just listen. It's up to you."

For the next hour I listened to the stories of all the women there. Each of them had lost a child to adoption. A few had even been reunited with the children they'd given up, but the majority were there to receive support as well as to give it.

As I told my story, the group listened in rapt silence. When I finished, one pretty blond woman spoke.

"Thank you for sharing, Fran. I'm Carol. We all know your pain, your shame, your confusion."

One by one, each woman validated my emotions and my experience. Some had been sent away to maternity homes to give birth. Some had been disowned by their families. Some had never told anyone in their families what they'd been through. Some had married the fathers of their children, and some had never married. Some had married and divorced other men. Some went on to have many children, while some never had any others. Our stories were all different, yet all the same. Finally, after all those years of silence, I had found a safe place to express my thoughts without fear of ridicule or shame.

The next day I went to work and found the letter from the Arizona Children's Home waiting for me. As promised, Marsha had sent along an authorization form. She had also enclosed a release of information form, in case I wanted to allow my child to contact me.

I immediately began filling out the form, but realized how much I didn't remember. What was my daughter's birthday? Was it March 4 or March 7? That was the week Grandma Ceil had died just two years later, and I could never remember which date was which. The form asked for the relinquishment date, but although it was two weeks after the birth, I couldn't be sure of the exact date. I filled it out as well as I could, put it into an envelope, and mailed it back.

The next Sunday, I went to the support group again. This time I spoke freely.

"I'm scared," I confessed. "I've never told my husband—we've been married almost twenty years. We have three children together. What if he hates me? How can I mess up my family that way?"

Trish, a tall, thin, attractive woman responded. "Secrets in families have a way of interfering with the life of that family. Even though you may never have said anything about your experience, it has influenced the kind of wife and mother you are. You've come this far; you can do this too. And remember this," she closed, "even if your husband supports you and handles it well, you don't owe him for that for the rest of your life."

I went home that afternoon full of resolve. I had to tell David the truth, and I had to let my children know what was going on with me.

That night, after dinner, David and I were preparing to go to bed. I started to cry and asked him to sit down. He looked stricken.

"Are you sick?" he asked worriedly. The words that had eluded me for as long as I'd known him came haltingly.

"Nothing like that, David. It's something that happened to me. Something I've always been too ashamed to talk about. And I'm afraid when I tell you—you'll hate me, or you won't love me anymore."

"I love you, Fran. It will be okay," he promised. "What is it?"

I started, "When I was seventeen, I . . . I had . . . a baby. My parents sent me away with Grandma Ceil and Grandpa Irving, and made me give her up for adoption."

David moved closer and held me in his arms while I cried.

"I'm so sorry I never told you, but I couldn't."

"Of course I still love you," he assured me, "but you'll have to give me a little time to process this. What about the kids? Are you going to tell them?"

"I understand completely. Take whatever time you need," I told David. "I have to tell the children the truth. They know I haven't been myself, but I can't live with the lies anymore. I have to find her, David. I have to make sure she's all right, and let her know the truth around her birth."

The next afternoon, after school, I called Alexis and Jay into my room. Corey wasn't scheduled to be home until later, so I decided to tell the two younger children first. I put it into the simplest terms I could. They were thirteen and eleven—so how much could they process? They were at a tender age and I wanted to do this right.

"I have something to tell you both that I've never shared with you before." I paused, taking a deep breath, and tried to choose the perfect words.

"When I was in high school, I had a serious boyfriend, and I got pregnant." They watched me carefully and didn't utter a word, as I continued. "My boyfriend wasn't Jewish, and Grandma and Poppi thought we were too young to get married, so they sent me on a long trip with Grandma Ceil and Grandpa Irving. We went to Arizona; I had the baby there, and then I had to give her up for adoption. In those days, it was a shameful thing for an unmarried girl to have a baby. I was very, very sad."

"Oh, Mommy," Alexis chimed. "That's the saddest story I ever heard." She hugged me tightly. "I'm sorry that happened to you."

Jay looked pale. He figured this would be a good time to confess some of his own sins, and he began to tell me about things he had done wrong—things I hadn't known about. Of course, those things were not important, so I smiled and let it pass.

"Mommy, that means I have an older sister. I've always wanted a sister. When are we going to meet her?" Alexis asked excitedly.

"We have to find her first. I don't know anything about her. There is a social worker in Arizona who is sending me some information, and as soon as I learn how to use it, we'll start to look for her."

When Corey came home a couple of hours later, the other two were squirming with anticipation. They met him at the door and corralled him.

"Mommy wants to talk to you. Go see her right now!"

Their mood was light, but Corey's was suspicious. He would be sixteen in a couple of weeks. How would he handle this? What would he think of me—his mother—who had been in a sexual relationship when she was not much older than he was now? Would it taint his view of me? Would he find the idea of me with a man other than his father repulsive? Telling Corey was even more difficult than I had imagined.

So I began my story, in much the same way I had with the other children. When I finished, he looked at me with compassion. "That's sad, Mom."

"You don't think less of me?" I asked.

"Of course not. What happened to you before doesn't mean you're not a great mother to us."

"You're not the oldest anymore, Cor," Jay taunted.

"Stop that, Jay. He is my first son, and the first child I raised. I love you all just as I always have, and I hope that when we find your sister, she'll let us love her too."

I had one more person to tell. I needed to confess the truth to Ken. He had to know I had given birth to his child. The following Monday, my heart pounding, I called him at work. "Ken, it's Fran. How are you?"

"Fine, Fran, good to hear from you. What can I do for you?"

I was so stressed, I could barely get the words out. Timidly, I spoke. "There's something I need to talk to you about. Can I come by your office one day after school?"

"Sure," he said. "How about day after tomorrow?"

"OK, that will work for me. About three o'clock?"

"Great, see you then."

I hung up the phone, still trembling. On Wednesday I would say the words that had waited nearly twenty-six years to be said. How would I get through this? How would Ken respond?

On Wednesday morning, I woke after a fitful sleep. Today was the day I would tell Ken. I dressed carefully. I wanted to look mature, pretty, yet serious. I chose a black pencil skirt and a blue silk blouse, and accented it with a beautiful necklace of crystal hearts suspended from a silver chain.

The day dragged by, and finally it was time. I walked into the school office and let one of the secretaries know that I had an appointment with Ken. He greeted me and escorted me into his office. He moved behind his desk and motioned for me to sit in the chair across from him. He could see how serious and nervous I was, and showed no emotion on his face.

"How are you, Fran?" he opened.

"Um, I'm here because I need to talk to you about something." I kept going because I had to.

"When people ask me how many children I have, I always say three. But the truth is, I have four. We had a child, Kenny, and my parents made me give her up for adoption." There—it was out. I finally took a breath.

He remained serious, but not surprised. "I always suspected, but you never said the words . . . "

He paused, gathering himself together. "There were rumors and questions back then, and I even told my father I thought it was why you went away, but I couldn't know for sure."

"What would you have done if I'd told you?"

"I would have married you, of course," he stated without wavering. His words hung in the air like a dark cloud between us. He said it so unhesitatingly that I knew it was true. He HAD loved me. I wasn't wrong about that. Part of me felt validated, part of me felt unmitigated sadness at what our lives were now and what they could have been.

"I was a different person then," I defended. "My parents wouldn't let me talk to you. I had someone watching my every move. All I wanted to do was have you rescue me, and that was impossible. I am so sorry."

"So why are you telling me now?"

"I have to find her . . . so she knows who she is. I have to know she is all right, that she is loved, that she is okay. I have to do this."

"I never told my wife about this, Fran. She knows we dated, but not this. She isn't going to be happy about it, but I will tell her. I'm not thrilled you are searching for her, but I know I can't stop you. Just let me know when you find her."

The air was thick with tension, and it was time for me to go. "Of course I will, Kenny. I'll keep in touch."

Shortly after that I received the information I had requested. It was a four-page document with non-identifying information about the adoptive parents, about my daughter's older brothers, and about her first year of life. It described her parents as warm and giving, an educated Jewish couple who were not all that different from my own family. I was ecstatic to learn how child-centered and loving they were.

The notes described her as pretty with reddish curly hair. Her parents thought she was beautiful and couldn't get enough of her. Every note related to subsequent home visits had the worker gushing about how she was doted on. One comment noted that she was a perfect baby who was always smiling and cooing. When she was nine months old, the worker described her as "one of the warmest, most responsive children" she had ever encountered.

I pictured my perfect baby and wanted nothing more than to hold her and tell her I loved her. But despite the thrill of learning about Molly as a baby and about her adoptive family, I still did not know her last name or where she lived.

I sent a note to Ken at work with the simple words: *Her name is Molly Beth and her birthday is March 7.*

EXCERPTS FROM MY JOURNAL

January 4, 1990

My Dear Molly Beth,

Your name—I toss it around my mouth and taste it, perhaps it will help me to taste the essence of you. Molly, what a beautiful, perfect name. You have a name; how ordinary that concept may seem to others—but not for me. The fantasy of my lost child, the emptiness of losing you, is replaced with the reality of your being, of the warmth that a name can bring.

Oh, to reach out and touch your face, your hair, to look into your eyes, to hear your voice, to hold you close to me . . . how long have I dreamed of the time when I would be able to do that. And that time now seems to be nearly within my grasp.

The memories I buried for so long, because I didn't feel I had a right to them, are returned to me. I want so much to set things right, to tell you how much I love you, that I have always thought of you, and prayed that you were happy and in a loving family— and I was sorry for any pain I might have caused you in your life, either through omission or commission.

I am here for you now, and always will be. I love the sound of your name, Molly, and I am eager to have you as a part of my life.

January 22, 1990

. . . I have never regretted loving your birthfather or giving birth to you. That experience made me all the more sensitive to the joy of life, of love, as well as to pain and suffering of others. I am available to give you whatever you might want from me—be it knowledge of your genetic heritage, or much more. Your parents were described as wonderful, loving, giving people. I hope you are fortunate enough to still have them with you.

Please know that there is another family who thinks of you often and has enough love to stretch across the miles, across the years, and across our extended families.

Can you forgive my youth, my acquiescence, my fear? Will you give me the opportunity to give you the only gift I can now offer— my love and friendship—the bond of love I have carried inside me all these years? I will search until I find you. I will wait as long as I have to—to earn your love.

And so began my journey. I continued to find comfort in the support group and validation with my therapist.

Day by day, I contacted my closest friends and family members and began sharing my story with them. At the beginning, I was terrified when I considered how I would be perceived. But each time I told my story I became stronger. Times had changed. This was 1990, and the world was used to single parenting. Teenaged mothers stayed in school and weren't shunned. People didn't whisper about premarital sex anymore. It was a different world.

Telling my mother was not easy. We were sitting in her kitchen when I broached the subject. "Mom, remember how you always said the worst thing in the world was to lose a child?"

"Yes, I don't know how parents can go through that. It's not the natural order of things."

"Well, Mom, that's what happened to me."

"What do you mean?" she replied with obvious confusion.

"When I gave up my baby, it was like a death. Only I wasn't allowed to know anything about it. I wasn't allowed to tell anyone or grieve."

"Oh, Fran, that's different," she defended.

"No, Mom, it's not. I lost a child. I gave birth and never saw my child again. You and Daddy said I would come back home and resume my normal life. But, Mom, I never forgot. I've tried, and it's with me every day of my life. I have a daughter, and I've decided to try and find her."

"I don't understand, Fran. But I suppose you'll do whatever you want to do," she declared defensively.

"I wish I could help you understand. It's something I have to do. I can't live with secrets or lies anymore. I have to tell the truth. It's part of me, part of who I am. If people don't respect that, then they don't really care about me."

At that moment I realized—my mother needs me in her life. She'll have to come around, or she'll lose me. I'm an adult now. I don't need my parents' permission to run my life. Revealing my secret was the healthiest thing I could do. I had to discharge my shame. When I found my daughter she was NOT going to be a secret. I could never do that to her. When I found her, she was going to find her first mother to be a healthy, strong, and admirable woman. That was my promise to Molly. That was my promise to myself.

With the information the agency sent me, I started contacting people and doing research. Tucson had three synagogues in 1964. I would call each of them to see what information I could gather. With my heart racing, I started the phone calls, and asked questions that related to the information I had. On one occasion I got a cantor on the phone and gave him misleading information about the reason for my questions, and I felt that I had reached an all-time low. I decided I would never do something like that again.

I had numerous talks with David about what I was going through. I felt an urgency I had never experienced before.

"David, I need to hire a searcher," I told him. "I have the name of someone in Arizona who is a professional and will help solve this mystery for us."

With David's blessing, I contacted the searcher. I gave her all the information I had about the family, and she promised to get back to me as soon as she could find out any new information. But she gave me a search tip, too.

"There is a Jewish Federation newspaper that comes out twice a month in the Tucson area. Why don't you put an ad in there and see if anything happens?"

That's a great idea, I thought. And so I composed a notice to be placed in the Federation newsletter as well as the Arizona Post and USA Today around the time of Molly's birthday.

> *BIRTHFAMILY EAGERLY*
> *SEARCHING FOR*
> *MOLLY BETH*
> *Born 3-7-64*
> *Tucson Medical Center*
> *Call Fran (203-XXX-XXXX)*

On March 7, I wrote in my journal:

> *How many wished you a Happy Birthday today? Was it happy? Was there a special lunch or dinner, flowers and cards?*
>
> *Among the many who love you—who sent messages of caring and wishes for a wonderful future—was one who couldn't reach you.*
>
> *And though I have no way of letting you know, I hope your heart is full and that somehow you can feel the one who gave you life will eternally be with you.*
>
> *I felt alone today—alone as always, with the pain of my surrender. Alone with the void of my loss. Terrified of knowing, and of not knowing.*

Alone with the ache—with the yearning to reach back across the years—when you were safely held within my body and my heart.

I brought home fresh tulips to give me comfort in my loneliness—for no one but Molly's mother remembered.

Molly's birthday came and went without a response to my ad. The searcher in Arizona called to report that she had a few good leads and would be getting back to me very soon. I continued my support group and therapy sessions, driven to reach some kind of closure.

CHAPTER 20
Finding Molly—Finding Me

*M*onday night, March 26, 1990, I kissed David goodbye and went to my weekly Mah Jongg game at my friend Paula's house, about ten minutes away from mine. Mindy, Lynn, Paula and I had been playing together for more than fifteen years. We started our routine and had played for about half an hour when Paula's phone rang in the kitchen. She got up to answer it. "Fran, it's for you. It's David."

"Hi, honey, is everything ok?"

"Fran, she called. Molly just called!"

"Oh my God, really? What did she say?"

"She asked for you, and when I told her you were at a friend's home, she said she'd call back in an hour."

"I can't believe it! OK, I'll be home soon." I started to cry and began to tremble with excitement.

When I went back to the living room, three pairs of expectant eyes look at me, obviously wanting to know what happened.

Because I had told Mindy my story over lunch several weeks before, she said, "Is it what I think?"

"Yes, it was her!" I continued to explain to the other two women what happened. "It's a very complicated story, but when I wasn't quite eighteen, I relinquished a baby for adoption. I started to search for her several months ago, and she called me!"

By that point, we were all crying. Mindy finally said, "Fran, go home and get that call, I'll fill them in on the rest."

"I'm going, I'm going!" I raced home with plenty of time to spare, and anxiously awaited her call.

Right on time, the phone rang, and, adrenaline flowing, I answered it. The voice I had been waiting to hear for more than twenty-six years was on the other end. It was a miracle, an answered prayer. She explained that in Tucson, friends of her parents had seen the notice I had placed in the Federation newsletter. They called her parents in California, where they had been living since Molly was two. Molly's father immediately called her to come over and talk about something important. When she arrived, he shared the notice with her, and told her that she could either wait until I found her, or she could respond and call me herself.

I was so happy Molly took the lead and called me. It set the tone for our relationship, and gave her some choices—choices she had been denied in the past. I decided then and there I would always let Molly take the lead in our interactions.

She was thrilled with having been "found," always wondering whom she looked like and if I thought about her on her birthday.

We had so many questions for one another, and before I knew it, more than an hour had passed. It was a joyful, yet overwhelming conversation, and the time came to say goodbye for now. I told her I would write and send pictures, and she said she would do the same. We exchanged addresses; she gave me her phone number, and we talked about reaching out again soon to make plans to meet in person.

David and the children were exploding with questions, and by the time I got everyone settled, it was after midnight before I could be alone with my own thoughts.

I sat down and wrote a letter I could finally send, and chose three pictures. One was of the seventeen-year-old me, one a current photo of me, and one a picture of me with David and the children.

> *Dear Molly,*
>
> *It feels so wonderful to be writing to you and know that this is one letter you will truly receive and read. I've written so many words to you I've tucked away—composed so many more in my head—all waiting for the day when there was hope of a response.*
>
> *Talking to you earlier this evening was a dream come true. It was a fantasy for so many years, and it makes me happier than words can express that you are interested in knowing me.*
>
> *I want to be honest and open with you about everything. I am generally quite open about my feelings, but this reunion path is uncharted territory, and I want it to go well.*

. . . I've always worried I wouldn't be able to find you, and knowing you are alive and well and have a loving family is what I've always hoped for. There is so much I want to tell you, so much I am anxious to learn about you. I don't want to overwhelm you with this first letter—but I am bursting with joy and excitement about this new phase of my life—our lives.

You sound like a very special young woman, and I look forward to getting to know you. I'll be in touch again very soon—and hope that you will be contacting me, too.

Love, Fran

The following week I received a beautiful note from Molly, complete with lots of pictures. She explained that she and her Mom had sat down and chosen photos that would show her growing from a baby to the adult she was now.

The photos did not disappoint me. Every one showed a beautiful girl who looked like me from the nose up and had her father's mouth. It was disconcerting to look at her pictures, knowing there was no doubt she was ours, and yet not ours. Yet, here she was, the baby gone, the woman a reality.

Molly at age 3.

I called Ken to tell him I had heard from Molly. He asked a few questions, and I offered to come to school to show him the pictures and letter she had sent. We met again several days later, in the late afternoon, when the building was sparsely populated.

"Let's go down to the break room to get a drink," he suggested.

I followed him into the room and sat at one of the round tables. He got a can of soda, but I only wanted water because my mouth was so dry.

"So tell me about her," Ken urged. I told him as much as I could remember, and pulled out the photos to show him. He saw my excitement, yet remained outwardly restrained himself. When our conversation had exhausted itself, we both became quiet and pensive. I rose from the table, and he followed my lead. As we headed to the door, I spoke.

"Kenny, how did you stop loving me?" I asked.

Without a moment's hesitation, he replied, "I had to."

Molly at about age 8.

"Would you just hold me for a moment?" I implored him.

With that, he took me in his arms one last time. Neither of us spoke, but I had no doubt that what we had so many years before was real.

CHAPTER 21

Reunion—Making Memories

*W*hen I gave birth to my other children, I experienced a different kind of joy. There was a continuity, an immediate love of them as an extension of myself as well as an ongoing intimacy. With Molly it would evolve very differently. I had always loved her because she was a part of me. But I found myself learning to love her in another way. I fell in love with the person she is. As I got to know her better over time, I loved her personality, the way she spoke, the way she loved her family and her friends, her self-knowledge, her beauty, the passion she had for her work. When she told me about things that were painful to her, I hurt too. It was a fascinating and tender learning experience to actually fall in love with her as my adult child.

After more phone calls and letters we decided to meet over a long weekend in early May. I made arrangements to stay with my father's cousin Arlene, who lived in Los Angeles. Arlene had a tiny place, but she was happy to allow me to sleep on her sofa. On May 3, I flew to California. I was so excited I could barely contain myself.

Arlene met me at the airport, and we drove back to her little apartment. As I unpacked, I carefully curated the outfit I would wear the first time I saw my oldest child. I was to meet her at her job, a retail shoe store in Beverly Hills, at closing time. I wanted to look like a perfect New York sophisticate, but radiate the warmth that would draw her to me. I wanted her to be proud that I was her mother and happy to learn more about me.

I was terribly nervous when Arlene dropped me off across the street from the store. Here I was in Beverly Hills, three thousand miles and twenty-six years from home. And my daughter was mere feet away from me.

I took a deep breath and entered the glamorous shoe boutique. I had waited my whole adult life for this moment, and it was finally here. There were two beautiful young women standing at the desk—but I had eyes for only one. My daughter, my Molly—a halo of striking auburn hair surrounded her eerily familiar face. She was dressed in a stylish black jumpsuit that looked as if it had been made just for her. I was totally entranced.

I slowly walked toward her, my heart pounding wildly. My mouth was dry, and I couldn't speak. We cautiously embraced, and I felt as if I would break into a million pieces if I moved from that spot. We finally separated, beaming, and looked into one another's eyes. There were so many unanswered questions, so many years of not knowing the other, yet my connection to her was certain. I could only pray that she would feel something similar.

Her friend Bari spoke, "I'm going to go now, you two. Have a wonderful evening. Molly, I'll see you tomorrow." And with that, my daughter and I were alone for the first time.

"Let me close up around here, and then we can go to dinner. Why don't you look around the shop a little while I do that," she offered.

My face was beginning to hurt from the enormous smile frozen there. "Of course," I rejoined. "The store is beautiful."

A few minutes later, we were sitting in her sporty white Toyota Celica convertible. She looked every bit the radiant California girl.

At our first meeting, May 1990.

"Let's go to The Cheesecake Factory here in Beverly Hills," she offered. "It's close by, the food is good, and we can sit and talk."

"That's fine," I replied. I was so nervous I didn't have much of an appetite, but whatever made her happy would make me happy. The restaurant was typical Mediterranean style with dusty peach faux paintings on the walls, a massive room with two-story ceilings. The hostess seated us at small table for two near a quiet corner. We faced each other across the table, and had an impossible time not staring. It was so hard to believe . . . it was surreal . . . was this a crazy dream, or had my most fervent wish actually come true?

"What do you usually eat here, Molly?" I inquired.

"They have great salads," she informed me. "I like the Chinese Chicken Salad or the Taco Salad . . . I think I'll order the Chinese Chicken tonight."

"That sounds perfect to me." I felt like such a hick—I had never had Chinese Chicken salad before. Actually, with three young children, I hadn't eaten lately in very many restaurants that weren't fast food or pizza. For the next two hours we sat and talked. Though the salad was delicious, I was so excited, I could barely get the food down. Molly asked questions, I asked questions, and we began to share who we were and what our lives were like.

It was impossible to catch up on twenty-six years in one night—it was too overwhelming and too new. Even in the years since, every conversation is fresh, every experience an exploration. I sadly learned that I can never recapture those lost years. Our relationship has had to develop over time—built upon her willingness to explore and experience her life with me as part of it.

That night, I told Molly about the souvenirs I had purchased in Tucson when I was pregnant with her. As my first gift to her, I gave her the little silver thunderbird charm I had bought so many years ago, and had worn on a chain around my neck every day since I started my search for her.

Molly drove me back to Arlene's apartment and we hugged good night. We would share dinner again the following night with her close girlfriends who wanted to meet me. I ran up the steps to the apartment filled with emotion—love, joy, fear, excitement, all intermingled. I told Arlene about our wonderful dinner and then we both prepared for bed. Arlene went into her room and closed the door, leaving me on the sofa in the living room. I turned off the light and let the events of the day wash over me.

Then the grief came. It stole into my soul, into my heart, and I began to cry. It was a primal cry—born of years of fear, of shame, of loss. I cried until there were no more tears, and then I slept.

The next morning, my sister's friend Gene drove me around Los Angeles and showed me the sights of the city. What could be better than my own personal tour guide? I hadn't been there since the spring of 1964, and it had changed substantially from what I remembered. Being there as a grown woman was a far cry from the scared almost eighteen-year-old who had been there with her grandparents. I absorbed the beauty of the terrain—the hills and canyons, the magnificence of the Pacific Ocean. I was astonished by the grandiose opulence of many of the homes that were a sharp contrast to the restraint of New England architecture.

Soon it was time to meet Molly and her friends for dinner. Arlene let me borrow her car, and I easily found my way to the upscale Italian bistro where they were waiting in the lounge. I wore a simple yet stylish black pant suit and heels, wanting to look sophisticated but still approachable. It was so important to me that Molly's friends approve of me. If they liked me, perhaps she would too.

Six pairs of eyes greeted me as I took my seat at the table. Her friend Bari, whom I had met at the shoe store, was there, as was her best friend since kindergarten, Dena. The other young women were obviously very close friends, but there were so many names to remember! Soon they were chatting with me as if I was one of the girls. Molly's friends excitedly asked me questions about myself and watched me closely. I was so nervous that I picked up my cocktail napkin and began playing with it. Before I knew it, it was in shreds. At that point, Dena turned to Molly and noted with amusement, "Molly, she tears her napkin just like you do!" We all laughed, and the ice was broken.

After that, the group engaged in a mad search to find all the ways Molly and I were alike. All her friends agreed that we looked very similar and had the same hair texture. We were both left-handed and were surprised to learn that we wore the same brand of perfume! Some of our mannerisms echoed one another, and I felt unadulterated joy that my long-lost daughter and I had so much in common.

The evening sped by and soon it was time to go. I drove home with a sense that things had gone well. However, I would be spending the next day with Molly's parents. This felt like it would be the real test. If they were okay with me—if they gave me their endorsement—I might have a chance to be part of her life in the future.

I arrived on time the next morning for breakfast. As I got out of the car I noticed her home was very much like the house I had grown up in. A California style ranch, it looked well cared for and inviting. Molly's Dad, Bernie, answered the door with a warm smile and a hug.

"Come on in. We're so happy you're here."

I held back slightly, but followed him into the great room, where the smells of the coming meal brought some comfort to my churning stomach. Molly came out of her bedroom and greeted me warmly, ushering me into the kitchen to meet her Mom. Eileen enthusiastically accepted the flowers I brought for her and immediately put me at ease. A tiny woman in her early sixties, with short gray hair, she reminded me of the way my beloved grandmother Ceil looked. Her smile lit up her entire face, and her cheerful countenance made me feel like everything would be okay.

Over a delicious menu of baked French toast and coffee, Eileen asked all the right questions. I felt comfortable sharing about my family and especially my children—mother to mother and her ease with herself was an inspiration to a very insecure me.

Molly and her parents, reunion weekend, May 1990.

Molly had to go to work, so Eileen suggested we go to a museum for the afternoon.

"I think you'll enjoy it. The Norton Simon Museum in Pasadena has Renaissance Art all the way through contemporary pieces."

"I know I'll enjoy it, Eileen. Let me help you

clean up, and we can go." Allowing me to help in her kitchen enabled me to feel like I wasn't just a formal guest.

When we walked through the museum, Eileen's observations and commentary matched well with what I had learned in college when I had studied art history. By the time the afternoon was over, I was energized by all we had shared. I believed I had made a good friend. We drove back to their home and Eileen invited me into her kitchen to help her prepare dinner.

As we worked, she told me all about Molly and her brothers' childhood adventures. She told me how the boys had adored her when she was a baby, and what a good and happy child she had been. She told me that her philosophy of child rearing had been shaped by the fact that she and her husband knew little about their children's birth families. There were no expectations about what their children "should" be like or what their aptitudes or talents might be.

"So we just let them be themselves."

I immediately thought of all the expectations I had for the children I was raising. I wondered if maybe having those expectations was not such a good thing. Maybe in her wisdom, Eileen was helping me to be a better mother. She was the kind of mother I aspired to be.

I wished that my parents had been so wise. It wasn't that they hadn't done their best—I absolutely understood that they tried to. But they were young and the only parenting model they had was what they, themselves, had grown up with. They never had the opportunity to be philosophical about parenting. They just did it.

After a comfortable family dinner, Molly offered to drive me to the airport the next day, and I readily agreed. I hugged Eileen and Bernie good-bye, and felt the genuine warmth and acceptance they exuded. I knew that I would see them again and sincerely looked forward to keeping in touch.

As I said goodbye to my newly found daughter, both of us looked forward to her visiting Connecticut at the end of June to meet her brothers and sister and the rest of our family. Bolstered by the memory of a wonderful weekend, I felt both content and elated.

I returned home to lots of hugs, kisses and questions about my visit with Molly. I felt like a new person. Alexis beamed with pride at the prospect of meeting her new big sister. The boys were a little more quizzical about what this new addition to the family would mean to them. I think everyone was a bit concerned that I had changed so much.

Mom wasn't thrilled with the prospect of "her" secret unleashed. The entire search and reunion process was so alien to her, so inexplicable, she couldn't comprehend what it meant to me. Not only did she not understand why I had to do it, she still had not dealt with her own shame and guilt over my pregnancy and relinquishment.

I began to plan for Molly's upcoming visit on the third weekend in June. Molly was to fly in on Thursday. Friday we would have a leisurely day together, and on Saturday we would have a family get-together with Mom, my sister, my nieces, aunts and uncles and a few very special cousins. I hoped Molly would not be overwhelmed, and I coached her on who everyone was and their relationship and importance to me.

Another event was scheduled for Sunday—my sister-in-law was to be married in my backyard. It would be a small wedding with just immediate family. Yet all my children would be there—a family event; for the first time in my adult life, my family would be complete. I am sure Molly did not fully comprehend the significance of that, yet she was a trouper and hung in there, meeting all those strange faces over two days and trying to sort out how she fit in.

Spending a day together in Connecticut.

Before she arrived, Molly and I spoke about whether or not she wanted to meet her birth father. She was nervous about it, but she asked me to call Ken and set it up. We arranged to meet him at school late on Friday afternoon. Most everyone would be gone from the campus, and we would have privacy and the opportunity to talk.

Being together was awkward for the three of us. Mostly Ken and I talked. I tried hard to include her in the conversation. We spoke about the old days—his family and mine, the places we enjoyed going and the things he enjoyed doing. This was our shadow family—the family that never was. The "what ifs" went unspoken, yet they were there none-theless. The two of them

All my children together, June 1990, Norwalk, Connecticut.

exchanged photos, and that was it. It was obvious there would be no further contact between them, and I was heartbroken for her.

In all the photos of the weekend of Molly's visit, I am beaming. Everyone is smiling for the cameras, full of joy at the enormity and importance of our new-found relationships. There is, however, one photo from that weekend with Molly in the background, and she is looking down contemplatively. She looks beautifully peaceful, yet alone, and I often wonder if she was overcome with the enormity of it all.

Even when Molly returned to California, I remained blissfully happy. It was all I could do to hold myself back from calling her often. Everything I had learned in my support group told me to give her the reins in the relationship and let her set the pace. I knew instinctively that she would need time to process it all, but I needed to let her know how much I loved her. I found greeting cards to send once a week or so, letting her know I was thinking of her, how important she was to me, and how much I cared.

In retrospect, I was falling in love. I often think about what it means to love one's children. When I gave birth to the children I raised, it was easy. I automatically loved them. They were born to me. I held them. I nursed them. I took care of them. They cried and I comforted them. They smiled their first smiles at me, and responded when I smiled at them.

This was different. I knew I loved Molly the minute I saw her. Yet getting to know her as a person was a vastly different process than with my other children. And so, the other part of love—the "I know who you are part"—came to me like a powerful new affair. I had to integrate the two parts of that love.

Even now, several decades later, I feel the power of that love, and I never take it for granted. Molly still manages the pace of our relationship, and it will always be that way because I never want to risk losing her again.

In September of that year, I began graduate school to become the counselor I was always destined to be. Three years later, I began my career as a school counselor for adolescents, and found my true calling. It was the best career choice I could ever have made. My work with teenagers allowed me the opportunity to help so many young people. I had learned a great deal from my experiences, and to me it was an honor to help my students find the tools to traverse their own life challenges.

In October 1990, I attended my twenty-fifth high school reunion. I was bursting with excitement. It was the time for me to fully emerge from my hidden life and share my joy with my former friends and classmates who had not yet heard my news. I told my story and showed Molly's picture to everyone who showed an interest. I was a new mother showing off her baby. I was energized even more by the positive and happy responses I received.

One of the people at the reunion was my friend Donna, whom I had not seen in many years, and she was very happy to spend the evening reminiscing. She had married Ken's closest friend Bob after graduation. We had gone out together many times, and she was there the night I saw him with another girl at the basketball game. When Bob heard the story, although I had not mentioned Ken's name, he put two and two together and was in a state of shock.

"He never told me," he said. "After you left town, we figured you might have been in trouble, but no one ever knew for sure, and he just didn't talk to me about it. He's very private, and after all this time, he still hasn't mentioned a thing. I'm very happy for you, Fran."

I was disappointed to hear that Ken was so closed off to sharing his emotions and his concerns with even his closest friend, but that was his issue, and I refused to let it diminish my elation.

The following December, Alexis and I traveled to California for a long weekend. We planned to spend as much time with Molly as her work schedule allowed. We also wanted to do some sightseeing, and it was important for me to help Alexis believe she was included in our family adventure. I worried about Alexis' feelings often. She had gone to our support group meetings, journaled her thoughts about having a new sister, and despite being only eleven years old, had been wrestling with some very strong emotions. This trip would be important for Alexis to see how she fit into this new version of our family, to see that Molly was also a part of another family, and to spend some special time alone with me.

It was a wonderful trip. Molly took some time off to go to Disneyland with us. I stepped back and let them experience each other. They rode rollercoasters (I wouldn't), and enjoyed the food, the music, and the excitement together. I was overjoyed to have them both with me.

While Molly was at work, Alexis and I went to a taping of the TV show "Who's the Boss." Courtesy of Sidra's old friend Gene, a producer, we got to meet the stars, and took lots of photos on the set to commemorate the event. Alexis looked adorable wearing her trendy pant suit with big shoulder pads. I'm sure she felt every bit the star as she posed on the stage. After that, we drove to Beverly Hills and walked Rodeo Drive, taking in the posh shops and the fancy cars. At the end of it all, she was a very tired, yet happy little girl. Our visit with Molly was fulfilling, and the trip a success.

My children and I continued to stay in close touch with Molly over the next year and a half. Alexis would soon be turning thirteen, and we were preparing to celebrate her coming of age in the Jewish tradition, with a Bat Mitzvah ceremony. Alexis let it be known how much she wanted her older sister there, and I couldn't imagine the celebration without Molly there.

When we were deciding the "honors" we would give out for the ceremony, Molly was a logical choice for one of them. I asked her Hebrew name, and she told me she didn't think she had one. I realized that Molly had been brought up in a synagogue with different traditions from mine, and had never been given a Hebrew name. Her mother graciously invited me to choose one for her. I was so excited—my first daughter would be called to the Torah by a name I would give her.

I studied Hebrew names for days—until I found one that resonated with me. Her name would be Mira—after my father whose Hebrew name had been Mordecai. There were many meanings given to Mira, but the one I liked best was associated with light. It seemed perfect to illustrate my coming out of the darkness in my life to the radiance that she exuded.

Alexis' ceremony and celebration, in August of 1992, could not have been more perfect. I was so proud of my little girl—now on her way to womanhood—and her teenaged brothers, so handsome and ready to take on the world. Molly was here, and all my children were with me.

CHAPTER 22
Loving and Losing

*O*ver time, Molly and I settled into a comfortable friendship. We would call one another intermittently to see what was going on, and I would try to visit during the summer when I could get away from work. The ache inside me for what I had lost never went away, but I got used to it as the price of gaining a relationship that was so much better.

In 1997, after Corey finished college, he moved to the Los Angeles area to pursue his dream of writing and producing screenplays. A year later, Jay moved out there too. Jay's plans were less concrete, but a group of friends decided to go there together, and it was exciting for him to be on his own so far from his comfort zone.

Alexis had had her fill of college by then, and in 1999 she moved to Atlanta with some friends and began her independent life as well.

During this time, my marriage began to crumble. After thirty years of being a supportive wife, I realized I was no longer the same woman I had been. I no longer needed the affirmation that I was a worthwhile human being, hiding in the safety of a marital security blanket. The things that were wrong in our lives were magnified by resentments, enabling, and a lack of hope for the future. In the fall of 2000, David and I sold our home and went our separate ways.

This was a sad time for me. After thirty years of trying to be happy, I had to get used to another new normal. I had tried my best to make our marriage work, but I had to admit failure.

As a single woman, I was not the same girl I had been in my early twenties when I needed validation. So, I found a lovely condo in a neighboring town, painted the inside lavender, and began to find out who I really was.

I had only myself to worry about. The children were pretty much launched, I had a good paying job as a counselor in a nearby school system. I spent hours learning how to be an expert on the computer and the emerging internet, and began dating again.

I was shocked when I received a call at work one day from my first high school boyfriend, Bill. He had tracked me down, and we chatted, recalling lots of our mutual friends and the innocent attraction we had once shared. He was coming to New York on business and wanted to get together. Single again himself, he was interested in the person I had become.

I was elated to see him. In a sweeping romantic gesture, he presented me with a single rose. We spent the next few hours getting to know each other again in a quiet restaurant. He gave me a gentle kiss goodnight, and said he would call me the next time he was coming to town. Over the next several months we did see each other and talk frequently on the phone. We settled into a nice, comfortable friendship, and the fog of my dead marriage began to lift.

I had a lot of dates after I became single again. Usually they were for dinner or coffee, and most were not great. But a few were interesting and I could analyze myself in the reflection of those new people.

I fell hard for one man whom I began dating in early March 2002. The first time we met, Artie and I felt fireworks. We quickly became inseparable. He took me away for my birthday to a beautiful bed and breakfast and we spent a leisurely couple of days antiquing, exploring the town, and walking hand in hand. In just a few weeks, he declared his love for me, and I was deliriously happy again.

In the interim, Molly had met her Mr. Right, and she and Danny were to be married at the end of April. Not only was I invited with Corey, Jason, and Alexis, but Mom was invited too. Mom was nervous about meeting Molly's parents, and I knew I would be on display for curious eyes.

I was unprepared but honored and grateful for the warmth and respect with which we were treated. We were invited into the room to watch as Molly and her husband signed their *Katubah* (the Jewish marriage contract), and from then on through the beautiful ceremony, my eyes were filled with bittersweet tears—tears of joy for how lucky I was to be in Molly's life, and tears of sorrow for all the time with her I had lost.

At Molly's wedding, April 13, 2002. Woodland Hills, California. Left to right: *Alexis, Jay, Danny, Molly, Me, Corey, Mom.*

Though I hadn't been fortunate enough to raise her, this beautiful woman was my daughter, and I would love her forever.

At the reception we were seated at a small table with Molly's parents and their good friends. I felt so privileged to be there with them, and as always, her mother made us feel special and wanted. When her father got up to make his speech toasting the newlyweds, he welcomed our family and thanked me for the precious gift of his daughter.

Molly's friends and their parents were equally kind, and I was content and appreciative of their thoughtfulness. Molly's new husband, Danny, couldn't have been more gracious, and treated me like I had always been part of their lives.

During the time I was in Los Angeles, Artie and I spoke every day. Our conversations were warm and eager, and even though I was having a great time, I was looking forward to going home to continue our relationship.

On Sunday, I called Artie as soon as I got home. "I'm back, honey," I said. "I can't wait to see you."

"I'm not up for it tonight," he replied. "Maybe on Tuesday."

"Okay, that's fine. Let me know. Is everything all right?"

"Sure, just had a tough week at work, and I'm really tired."

"Talk to you soon, love you."

"Love you too," he said.

But then Tuesday came and went with no call. And Wednesday, and Thursday. Something was definitely wrong. I called again.

"What's going on, Artie? Everything was perfect. I'm worried about you. Why haven't you called?"

"It's hard to explain. I can't do this. I just can't."

"I don't understand," I murmured.

"Give me some time," he insisted.

And I waited, and waited . . . and waited some more. It made no sense. He had told me he loved me. We had made plans for me to meet his daughters. Then, nothing.

I called a few more times, and he never answered. That was it—I had been dumped, never to find out why. I sank into a deep depression—couldn't sleep, couldn't eat. Foolishly, I had let my guard down, hoping to love again, and being gravely hurt in the process. For six months (longer than the relationship had existed), I analyzed and overanalyzed what had gone wrong. Finally, I concluded that he must have been afraid of his feelings, commitment, or me, and I chose to move on. I would be more careful next time.

Molly and Danny returned from their honeymoon and shortly thereafter announced she was pregnant. I was so excited for her—and for me! My role in her life was to become more complicated, and it would evolve in a way I was unable to predict. Would I be lucky enough to be "Grandma" to her baby? What would that mean? How involved could I be? What would that look like?

CHAPTER 23

Forever

The call came. On January 13, 2003, Molly gave birth to a healthy baby girl, and they named her Sydnie Morgan. This was my granddaughter, flesh of my flesh, a child whom I could watch grow from her birth for as long as I lived.

My winter break was six weeks later, and I flew to California to see Molly and meet Sydnie. Corey picked me up at the airport, and we drove straight to Molly's house. As we entered, excitement and nervousness washed over me. I so wanted it to be a perfect visit. I wanted to be welcomed and have Molly understand how important this visit was to me.

She immediately greeted me with a loving embrace. "Do you want to see the baby?"

"Of course I do!" I exclaimed.

"Come," Molly invited. "She's in her crib."

We entered the nursery, perfectly decorated with furniture painted a soft white, and fabrics in cream and pastel green. I saw the shock of dark hair and the tiny body swaddled tightly, and my eyes began to well with tears. My heart was exploding with joy.

"Do you want to hold her?" Molly asked.

"Oh yes, of course," I replied jubilantly. "Thank you."

She handed me the petite bundle and the aching in my arms went away. I was holding the most precious gift I have ever been given. I had never been able to hold Molly and look into her eyes, but now I was holding her daughter, my granddaughter, looking in HER eyes, and knew that this child felt all the love I had to give. I would always be there for her, always be someone she could trust, someone who would forever be in her life, someone who would forever be her Grandma.

EPILOGUE

This book has taken me twenty-seven years to write. The story has always been in my head, swirling images of the Fran from years past and the Fran of just yesterday. There isn't a day or an hour that goes by that I have not thought of *The Story of Molly and Me*.

It was hard to know where to end this tale, as it is ever growing. There are dozens more moments I could have recounted, and countless others I will experience with my family in the future. I ended here because I am certain the person I am today is the one I was ultimately destined to be. I believe that we are shaped by the things that happen to us in our lives and by how we respond to them. Only once in my life did I ever give up hope that tomorrow would be a better day. My friend Nancy rescued me that day, and while the road has not been easy, I try every day to see my glass as *at least* half full. At this point, "my cup runneth over"!

In the fourteen years since I first cradled Sydnie in my arms, life has been rich. In 2008, Molly and Danny were blessed with a son, Joshua, and I am the proud grandmother to that sweet, handsome young boy and amazing athlete. Sydnie is a beautiful young woman, inside and out, a talented dancer and an introspective thinker. Both the children are intelligent, warm and loving. To them, I am simply Grandma Fran. They are always happy to hear from me, and always tell me how much they love and miss me.

In 2008, I married Phil Vadeboncoeur, a wonderful, funny and devoted man, who has been my best friend and companion. We retired in 2013 and we have been given a bountiful life—filled with love and two energetic dogs! I have four wonderful children, two amazing grandchildren, and the love of many friends. Best of all, I get to love them too.

Holding baby Sydnie, February 2003.

Molly, 2016.

Above, left to right: *Josh, Danny, me, Phil, Molly, and Sydnie. February 2016.*

Left: *Molly, Sydnie, Danny and Josh. October 2012.*

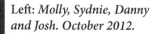

At Sydnie's Bat Mitzvah, February 2016. Left to right: *Jason, Phil, me, Corey, Alexis.*

Evening

A Bob Dylan record with a scratch
A train whistle and an ambulence siren
   far off in the distance
A party somewhere down the street
Snow falling lightly on the window sill
One tear sliding quietly down my cheek.

—Fran Gruss, 1966